FRE TO FAIL

SHABNAM AGGARWAL is an entrepreneur, advisor to social enterprise change-makers and author. The founder of varied high-impact startups, she is best known for her work advancing the education technology revolution in India. Her contributions have been featured on media outlets such as The *Times of India*, The *Economic Times*, The *Guardian*, The *Hindu*, Huffington Post, EdSurge, VCCircle, YourStory and Entrepreneur.com. Shabnam has guest lectured on entrepreneurship at universities including IIT, IIIT and MIT, and spoken at TEDx's around the world. She is a fellow of Summit, Sandbox, StartingBloc and Uncharted, and a former executive at Pearson and Merrill Lynch.

Having built three companies from scratch, Shabnam holds the irreplaceable experience of having failed numerous times in the startup world. She is passionate about debunking the stigma of failure, specifically for South Asian women who are often held to a different standard than the rest. *Freedom to Fail* is her first book.

Originally from Northern California, Shabnam lived in Cambodia for one year and India for seven years building companies and writing about her experiences. Shabnam's popular blog, blog.shabnamaggarwal.com, has tens of thousands of readers. She is an avid explorer who does not currently reside in one place, but readers can find her talking shop on Twitter or upside down practicing handstands on her Instagram account, both @shubbless.

SHABNAM AGGARWAL

FREEDOM TO FAIL

LESSONS FROM MY QUEST FOR START-UP SUCCESS

HarperCollins *Publishers* India

First published in India by
HarperCollins *Publishers* in 2018
A-75, Sector 57, Noida, Uttar Pradesh 201301, India
www.harpercollins.co.in

2 4 6 8 10 9 7 5 3 1

P-ISBN: 978-93-5302-313-3
E-ISBN: 978-93-5302-314-0

Typeset in 11/16.1 Stempel Garamond LT Std at
Manipal Digital Systems, Manipal

Printed and bound at
Thomson Press (India) Ltd

This is primarily a work of non-fiction. Some names, locations and details have been changed to protect people's identities. Wherever possible for me to confirm details, I have done so, but most of this book is based on my memory. Geoff Dyer once wrote, 'Memory has a spottiness as if the film was sprinkled with developer instead of immersed in it.' My story is true to my recollection of the events as they took place, but my confidence in the accuracy of my memory is impossibly high. I apologize in advance to anyone whose memory film does not match up with mine. Namaste.

For Sereena, and all the little girls out there; don't be afraid to fail. Be afraid to not.

'I continue to find my greatest pleasure, and so my reward, in the work that precedes what the world calls success.'

– Thomas A. Edison

Introduction

When I first started working on this book, I thought it would be one of those how-to-find-success-in-startups-and-in-life kind of books. I thought I'd write about how I overcame adversity and failure and stepped out of the startup boxing ring with my head held high and my chest puffed out, jumping around like Rocky Balboa in *Rocky III*. I thought I would have found the magical pot of success – gold at the end of the failure – rainbow by now. I thought I would tell you about how I did it and how you can too.

Then I started the research. I picked up one book after another that said exactly that: *10 steps to startup success! Follow these rules to build a great company! Here's how Steve Jobs did it. Learn from the best!* But I had read many of these books while I was building my startup, and none of them helped me one bit back then.

These kinds of books were all trying to give me, the entrepreneur, pointers, to help me see potholes before I stepped into them, and give me answers to questions I didn't have yet. None of them helped me avoid failure, though. Worse, every single one was written by someone who had ultimately succeeded to grow or sell their business. None of them shut down, walked away, nor admitted to colossal loss.

I realized there was no way to help a budding entrepreneur avoid failure. It was inevitable, it would be painful, and it was, in fact, necessary for each of us to go through. My failures were the hardest moments of my life, but they shaped me 100 times more than my successes ever did. Even the final one.

So, I knew I would have to write about failure in my book. How could I write about *my* failures though? I was raised to hide my failures in a dark corner and shine a light on my successes. That was how I would climb the imaginary ladder to enduring success. I couldn't possibly tell the world, or even you, the one person who stumbled upon this book amongst the hundreds of others on the Amazon and Flipkart shelves, that I had failed. What would people say?

What was worse was how painful it was to relive those memories of failure while writing my book. Every time I sat down to write a story about how I failed in hiring, marketing, sales, fundraising, leadership, friendship, or even firing people, my hands froze and my heart yearned for me to run away from the page.

I have always had a deep and debilitating fear of failure. But my fear of people knowing I had failed was even more paralyzing.

It turned out that my memories of my failures were what psychologist Ulric Neisser calls flashbulb memories – memories of shocking, emotional events that leave a particularly vivid imprint on your mind. William James, the father of American psychology, once described these imprints in 1890 as 'so exciting emotionally as almost to leave a *scar* upon the cerebral tissues'. The memories are so detailed and vivid that it's almost like a picture taken with a flashbulb, Elizabeth Phelps, a cognitive neuroscientist at NYU, says.

When I recalled the events that occurred while building my startup, I was scratching the scar tissue on my memory. Opening the wound up would hurt and talking about it on the page would feel almost as painful as living through the events in the first place.

However, research also shows that to recalibrate our brain to feel less extreme emotions of fear and pain with regards to an event, we need to explore the event. In fact, we need to explore it within what's called the vulnerability window. If we do, and if we do it right, we can recall the memory without experiencing the fear and emotions we once felt when the event occurred. We can even approach a similar event and feel no fear whatsoever.

That is how I wanted to feel about startups again. Writing each word, each page, each story of this book was my attempt to fall back in love with the starting up, building a business, failing at things, growing a team, and doing something meaningful with my life.

My hope is that over the next ten chapters of adventures in failure, we will both walk out of this boxing ring with our heads held high, our chests puffed out, and our fists up ready to fight the good fight again.

Prologue

My dear, incredible, beautiful team of superheroes,

Over the past two years, we have given this idea everything we've got. We've given it our love, our time, our sweat, and even some of our tears. We've showed up unannounced on doorsteps, we've bugged people at malls, cafes, and on the streets, and we've trampled through unknown territories searching for amazing teachers. We've reached out and held the hands of hundreds of thousands of parents as they navigate the murky and confusing waters of their kid's childhood. We've supported thousands of small business owners and teachers as they grow their classes and teach more kids their talents. We've even supported one another as we've grown and dealt with various personal and professional challenges, and we've truly thrived. We've become the true definition of a team:

a group of people who support and challenge one another through thick and thin, and stick together while growing in their own individual directions.

Some fun facts: Did you know we've made almost 6,000 direct connections between families and teachers across India? Did you know we've had parents visit us from 160 different countries and almost 3,000 different cities? (There are only 196 countries in the world, by the way.) Did you know that almost 50 per cent of our 3,60,000 users are actually dads? Did you know that 70 per cent of our users found us on their mobile phones and spent almost 1 minute using us? (That's a lot in thumb-time.) We've accomplished some amazing feats together, and come a long, long way from Day One, when we were hidden in the back-corner table of someone else's office!

We've also made mistakes though. Did you know I once accidentally deleted our entire photo database of 10,000 listings? Did you know we once spent a crazy sum of money on a radio ad that was never actually aired? Did you know we once almost burnt the entire office down by leaving a light on overnight?

We've struggled together to pick up from our numerous failures and we've walked through fire together, hand in hand, reaching great heights time and time again. Sometimes we faltered, sometimes we succeeded, but one thing I can say for sure is that we've never judged one another for trying, and that is a truly special culture we've built here at KleverKid that I am immensely proud of.

Unfortunately, every adventure must run its course, and every adventure has a beginning, a middle and an end. And this wonderful little adventure of ours has reached its end. I could try and list the reasons for why and how this adventure has reached its natural end, but I fear none of them can properly tell us what went right or wrong. Some might say it was purely external market factors: the market for startups has declined and we suffered from the impact. Some might say it was timing: we were too early (or too late) to enter a nascent and complex market. Some might say it was the idea: we were not focused enough (or too laser focused) to justify a scalable, sustainable product. Some might say it was the model: there is no proof yet that hyperlocal marketplaces work, profitably. Some might say it was me: I was too caught up in the expectations of selling a strong vision of the business rather than building a truly strong business.

We'll be shutting down by 12 August, which is next Friday.

We are offering you all salary for all of August and 100 per cent of mine and PK's support to search and help you find new jobs all through August. We have work to wrap up together, we have clients and users to call, so let's come in and hang out at the office while we sob and laugh and reminisce about the good times together. We'll ask some of you to work with PK on letting our users and clients know as soon as possible, some of you will work with me on handling the business and tech side, and we will make every effort to return the money to all incomplete contracts.

I am so incredibly proud of and forever indebted to each of you for putting your heart and soul into this business and family. We gave it all we've got, and there are no regrets at all.

I love you guys, and I am sorry to have let you down. I know it's my job to keep the dream alive, but I hope I can convince you that the big dream still lives within each of us. I hope I can count on you to continue to pursue this crazy big dream of helping kids discover their passion and changing the world.

Yours truly,
Shabnam

4 August 2016

Chapter One

'You choose: You can decide not to do interesting things...or you can count on failure.'

—Minnie Ingersoll, Founder of Shift

It all started back in May 2014. It was the hottest, muggiest, most oppressive day of the year in New Delhi. The electronic display on the street showed 45° Celsius, 114° Fahrenheit. When I stepped outside it felt like I was swimming through the dense wet air, cutting a path open ahead of me with my outstretched hands and kicking away the past with my paddling feet. It was my last chance, the final days in the first half of 2014, and I was painfully aware of the fact. I was twenty-eight years old. I hadn't accomplished much in 2014 so far. Most of it was spent wallowing in my apartment about the demise of my education consulting firm and fruitlessly trying to figure out what to do next with my life. I had expected more from myself by now.

I sat down in the backseat of a taxi, and I let my fear do all the talking in my head.

After a year of fits and starts over 2013, finally in January of 2014, my thirty-one-year-old Californian co-founder had decided it was time to call it quits with India. He left me and our fledgling two-person education consulting company in Delhi, to take a month-long Vipassana meditation in Nepal and then move back in with his Dad in Los Angeles so he could 'find himself' again. A few months later he would take a job with Google.

I didn't hug him goodbye, I didn't drive him to the airport, I didn't wish him well. I was angry. He wasn't just my co-founder; he was my best friend. This was my second attempt at building a business on my own, and my second failure, but this time I couldn't control it, I wasn't responsible for it, and yet, I still felt that I was.

I still felt the burning shame of failure turning my face red while rejecting my father's phone calls every day. I felt the awkward silence that followed after I nervously told an investor at a conference, 'Oh, my co-founder actually had to leave the country…personal issues…you know how it goes…no, I'm not sure when he'll be back…

no, not sure what I'll do with the business…it's just me now…so…I'll have to see…'

I felt that instinctual sigh of relief from other entrepreneurs who recognized my darting eyes and shifting feet, who had also been in the deep, dark hole as I was then, but who had faith I would climb my way out and see the light of hope and optimism once again.

Failure was inevitable, I told myself. Failure was important. Failure was necessary. This failure, every failure, would bring me one step closer to success, I said.

Then why does this feel so awful, I wondered. How would I climb out of this hole? What should I do differently next time to prevent this from happening again? How could I ensure I would never feel this way again?

The taxi stopped outside the entrance gate of a massive whitewashed building with four long, yellow buses parked side by side, inches away from one another.

I followed the lead of a seasoned old principal down the heavily air-conditioned hallway of her primary school as she pointed out the numerous achievements of her students in South Delhi. I had used my tried-and-true method to get her to meet me on that oppressively hot and muggy day in May of 2014: I told her I was an expert consultant in integrating technology with education in schools. Technology was a hit with most of the school principals I contacted – they were each competing to attract new families to their schools. Parents were mesmerized by shiny laptops, slick tablets and smart projectors with animations teaching the students about Gandhi and the Salt March, and principals knew it was the way to hook parents, even if they secretly believed technology added zero value to their students' education.

My motive in meeting this principal was not entirely clear to me that day – I was also secretly starting to believe technology, as it was being used in classrooms in those days, was doing more harm than good – but when I think back on it now, I realize I was feeling around in the dark to find the steps to climb out of my hole. I had always found my way forward in schools, hanging out with kids, feeding off their energy, passion and idealism.

As we shuffled down the hallway, I studied the bobby pins hidden inside the principal's bun, holding back her shiny dark black hair with immaculate precision. I noticed the way her pointy elbows moved ever so slightly when she gestured to an award protected by a glass case in a corner of the hall. I listened as, without missing a beat, she barked instructions to the various teachers that passed us in the halls, all the while sticking to script with me about her school. I admired the soft accent in her English as she said with pride, 'We ensure the low-income children in our community have space in our school as well.'

On a downbeat, as she spoke to a teacher in the hallway about an upcoming exam, a child dropped his pencil near my feet. I knelt to pick it up.

'Hello. What's your name?' I asked.

'Sorry, ma'am. Thank you, ma'am. Sachin, ma'am,' he mumbled.

'What class are you in?'

'Fifth class, ma'am,' he said.

'What's your favourite subject, Sachin?' I said.

'Subject, ma'am? Actually, I like cricket, ma'am. I am a great bowler,' he said with a hint of a smile.

'Wow! That's great,' I said. 'Do you play here on the school team?'

One beat. Two beats.

'No, ma'am. The coaching is too expensive here. I play behind my home with my friends.'

I thought back to my fourth year of high school when, finally, after years of trying and failing, I was voted by my coach, Mr Barth, and my teammates, to be the captain of my school's soccer team. My dad came to school for the announcement. The outgoing captain put a garland of flowers around my neck. It was the proudest moment of my teenage life, and over the course of the next year, I learned everything I knew about leadership, teamwork, and humility from Mr Barth. The experience laid the foundation for me to eventually become an entrepreneur.

Today, for the life of me, I could not recall how to take the derivative of a logarithm, but I can remember with surprising precision how difficult it was to convince my broken-hearted teammate to wipe her tears and take her anger out on the field against our opponents. She scored three goals that game.

'Do you have a coach?' I asked.

'No, ma'am. We just play for fun.'

'I see. Can you give your parents my phone number? Maybe I can try to find a coach for you.'

Confused, he took the torn piece of notebook paper with my name and number on it and darted off to class. I didn't know any cricket coaches at the time, and I definitely could not coach cricket myself, but I figured I could Google some coaches, call around, and find one or two that might be willing to coach a few kids from his area. Every kid deserved a great coach like Mr Barth, I thought to myself.

I stood up as the principal finished her conversation with the teacher. She continued with her script as we walked up the stairs to the second floor of the school. She walked me down an identical hallway, one floor above, pointing out a classroom where the students were taking an exam on tablets. We passed another room where the teacher was writing on the blackboard while two more women walked around the classroom, checking students' work. The smell of chalk reminded me of the first school I had visited in India, in 1993, when I was eight.

Mom and I were visiting Punjab for her nephew's wedding, but Mom had another agenda on her mind. Mom had left India for Silicon Valley back in 1976 when she was twenty-years-old to move in with her husband, my Dad, whom she had met once prior. That was how arranged marriages worked back then.

Coming back to India as a grown, married woman was Mom's opportunity to share her American wealth and give back to her community. Mom decided on our trip that she wanted to visit the elementary school she had attended as a child. She squeezed my hand tight as a man walked us through the drab grey school. The students sat on hard wooden benches that spanned the width of the room, with their feet dangling below and their elbows resting on the long wooden plank in front of them. They held the tiny nubs of their pencils with ease as they furiously copied down the teacher's notes from the blackboard. They were learning to read three letter words in the fourth grade. I tried to read one word on the board, 'wus', but didn't recognize it. I nudged Mom in the waist and pointed to the word on the board. Mom pulled me into the other room.

Now, the old principal had led me into her office and was offering me chai, with her middle finger on the buzzer on top of her desk, waiting for my response. I accepted, knowing the custom would give me time to ask my questions.

'Your school is very impressive,' I said to her. 'It looks like you've already got state-of-the-art technology in all of your classrooms with well-trained, highly qualified teachers. What can I do to help?'

'Yes, we have invested in all the latest technologies,' she said. 'But my fear is that all this technology is making the children very sedentary. They are hooked on to these gadgets throughout the day, and then they go home and stare at the TV or their tablet or their parents' mobile phones. Children used to play outside, have fun and find hobbies and interests they were passionate about. Now, they're stuck behind these devices and I'm worried they will never find an interest to pursue later in life. Even if it's engineering, at least they should be interested in it, rather than forced into it, only to leave engineering immediately after their studies are over. It's a waste of their education.'

'Are you giving them unstructured time during the school day?' I asked.

'We are, but it's not enough.'

'Are the parents putting them in afterschool classes?'

'It's expensive these days, hard to find good tutors and coaches, and parents don't want to drive in this crazy hot Delhi traffic for hours just to send their kid to a good art class or science tutor.'

'Do you think there's a way to offer cheaper classes at your school? I met a student downstairs who said it was too expensive for him to join the cricket coaching here.'

'We've tried but it's very hard. We rent out some of our spaces afterschool but the parents still find issues. They think we're trying to swindle them but we have no choice. It's very expensive to maintain the grounds.'

'I see. What about a newsletter? Could you recommend outside classes that way?'

'I don't want to seem biased. These afterschool programmes operate on very slim margins and there's a new one popping up every day. I don't want to take on that burden, I have enough going on in my day.'

'Aren't there any online websites where they list these programmes? Rate them? Show the price?'

'Nothing very good. Do you know of any?'

'I don't know much about the afterschool space – all my work until now has been inside schools,' I said to her.

'I see. But tell me one thing, your accent and your dress sound and look like you grew up in America. Why are you here, in India? Do you have family here? Are you married? Who do you stay with?' the principal asked me.

I thought about the moment I decided to move to India. It was August in 2009, at the end of the summer. I had been working in Cambodia at a social enterprise for a year, but feeling unsettled, like I hadn't found my home yet. Staring out the window that overlooked a decrepit old school-turned-genocide-prison-turned-genocide-museum called S21, I took a call with a professor from

Carnegie Mellon University. He told me about his research using educational cell phone games to teach English to kids in rural India. He said his games were ten times more effective in teaching English than the teachers teaching English in those same areas. He said he needed to find a social entrepreneur to move to India and build the business arm of his research with him, while he taught and researched out of Pittsburgh. In minutes, I was hooked.

That's me, I thought to myself.

I moved to Hyderabad two months later, in October of 2009, and fell in love with India immediately. *This is my home*, I said to myself. *These are my people. This is my problem to solve.*

I blinked away the memory and looked the principal in the eye.

'I moved here five years ago to work in education. My first and second education businesses failed, but India is my home now and I'm committed to giving children better access to a high-quality education. I have family in Punjab but I live on my own nearby, in Safdarjung Enclave. Let me see what I can find out for you for after-school programmes for your students. I am sure there's something out there that can help.'

I walked out of the principal's office that day wondering if I had just found my hammer and chisel to carve the first step into the wall of my dark hole. I had never thought about kids *after* school. I had only ever thought about what I could do for them *during* school. After school opened a sea of opportunities that *during* school limited; it was unregulated by the government, it was decentralized and run by smaller mom-and-pop shops, and my own mother had been running an after-school program teaching Hindi out of our garage in Silicon Valley for the past thirty years, but still struggled to grow.

It sounded like the exact same problem people faced when it came to discovering new restaurants, or hailing a cab, or finding a home to stay at during vacation. Yelp, Uber, AirBnB. Extremely successful companies had been built on these exact same premises. Had no one considered this solution for parents and their children's needs?

I went home and started my research. There was one small startup in the US doing something similar, and one in Delhi, but the user experience was awful and the information and photographs looked unappealing. The reviews seemed faked. Worst of all, they didn't show the fees for the classes. What good would AirBnB be if they didn't tell you the cost per night for a room?

I pulled out a piece of white paper from the printer and started sketching out what this website might look like. It would have a map, like AirBnB, show fees, and have big, beautiful, professional pictures of the afterschool programs. It would be easy to search and filter to make a parent's life easier. It would tell you how far the programmes were from your office or home. Only programmes that shared fees publicly would be listed – we would democratize the after-school space – hidden fees and under-the-table deals would be over.

I spent the next week barely sleeping, building mock ups, interviewing parents, creating and recreating business models, calling Mom to ask her what she would or would not pay for as a small business owner trying to grow to teach more children Hindi in Silicon Valley while keeping her fees affordable and accessible.

Any startup book will tell you that early customer research and validation should *not* be done with your own family and friends; they are inherently biased towards supporting your ideas. *Especially* your mom. But I couldn't help myself. My mom was the perfect merchant for this marketplace.

'I've tried everything to increase enrolment,' Mom said. 'I even bought ad space on the back of the local bus the other day, just to see if I might get some new business that way. It's so hard to find new students.'

'Would you pay a small fee for every new student if someone else was doing the marketing for you?' I asked feverishly.

'I definitely would,' she said. 'I don't want to waste my time with marketing. I'd rather teach more kids Hindi.'

Eureka! I thought. *This is it.*

I called my friend Gauri, who studied business at Carnegie Mellon and worked in finance on Wall Street, to have her look at the first business model. She also happened to be a new mom in India, and I knew she'd be honest with me.

'It's an interesting idea,' she said. 'I definitely depend on other parents' recommendations so much since there isn't any website here for me to find these things. I would still visit the location to make sure it was legitimate and safe, but it sounds like it could be super useful. There's always so many great kids' programmes available that I don't know about until after the fact! I would love a way to find out about all of them in one place.'

My hammer and chisel moved at rapid pace, working away to shape a step that I finally felt ready to climb up on, after months of motionlessness.

Then, I looked at my bank account. I had $1,000 (Rs 60,000) left. My rent, $400/month (Rs 24,000/month), was due in two days.

Chapter Two

'The first half of our lives is ruined by our parents and the second half by our children.' – Clarence Darrow

I knew I was running out of money, fast. I knew the smart path was to get a job that paid me well enough so that I could save up some money and then start this company on my own savings, on my own two feet. I could hear Dad's voice in my head saying those exact words. *Why the rush? It's too risky. Get a normal job!*

I had normal jobs before. But I figured that in India, it would take me years to save up the seed capital I needed to get this idea started. I couldn't wait years before starting this business – it was too critical, it had too much potential, and parents and children needed it now. I wasn't willing to leave my new home, my mother country, just to make some money. *What if I got caught up in the grind and never found my way back to India?*

I wanted to build a Yelp or JustDial for children's after-school programmes. I wanted parents to be able to open my website, type in anything their child was passionate about – be it karate, chess, painting, abacus, cricket, poetry, math, or underwater basket weaving – press enter, and be presented with a list of nearby options, the teacher's ratings, and the cost to sign up.

Based on my business model calculations, I needed fourteen lakh rupees to get me to the end of the year. With that, I could hire a couple teammates, pay my rent, find a small office space and build the beta version of the website to start testing it with parents. That would also buy me enough time to meet more established investors and raise a seed round.

Fourteen lakhs wasn't nearly a large enough sum to excite a normal venture capital investor though, especially when I was so early-stage with my idea. There was too much risk involved. According to *Forbes*, 90 per cent of startups failed. I needed to find someone who trusted me, believed in my abilities and who wouldn't bog me down with a tonne of legal work before I even got started, so that I could reduce that likelihood of failure and then approach VCs.

'What do you think I should do?' I asked KC, a long-time investor and close friend.

'You should try raising a "friends and family" round,' he said.

'How does that work?'

'Basically, you ask all your friends and family for the money and handle the details later, if things work out.'

If things work out, I repeated to myself.

The only people from my friends and family that would even consider this for a moment were my parents.

I had to think long and hard before asking my parents for money, though. I knew it would bruise my Independent Lady ego. They had spent a lot of money on my education already, and I was reminded more than once over the years that the point of my education was to give me the tools to survive and thrive on my own, not to borrow money from them until they went broke. That seemed like a fair stance in my rational mind, as well.

I wasn't feeling very rational at the time, though. I felt feverish, excited and unstoppable. I felt like Serena Williams searching for her racquet on game day.

I stared at the black cursor blinking on the blank, white screen of the compose mail window like an impatient clock ticking. *What do I do?*

'You have no other choice,' the sassy, know-it-all, alter ego in my head said to me.

'I could ask someone else,' my fear said back.

'Who else is going to loan you fourteen lakhs?'

'I could borrow it from the bank?'

'The bank will screw you. Or they'll say no. We both know that.'

'I cannot ask my parents. They will hold me hostage forever.'

'So, what? You'll have to show up to a few distant cousins' weddings and visit home instead of climbing Mount Kilimanjaro for the next few years. Big deal.'

'It is a big deal,' my fear said back. 'I need my independence.'

'What for?'

'To prove I have succeeded.'

'Have you, now?'

'Fuck off.'

'What are you *really* worried about?'

'What will Dad say if I fail?'

Dad would say failure is not an option. It didn't need to be said out loud though; growing up my elder brother, Yogi, and I just knew. We knew from the foreboding silence that fell upon the house just before Dad walked in the front door after work, sending us scurrying to our bedrooms to finish our math homework in silence. We knew from the 'The Rime of the Ancient Mariner' that Dad would read to us before we slept: *You don't want to be the one with an albatross around his neck.* We knew from the slight click of his tongue at dinner parties when he called us over to brag to his friends, reminding us not to go off script.

Dad would say, 'Shaboo! Come here, come here.' Turning to his friend, another dad at the party, with one hand gripping my shoulder and the other cradling a glass of pungent golden liquid with two cubes of ice, he'd say, 'You know what Shaboo's been up to these days? Tell him, Shab, tell him. She just got an award in her school's science competition! You won't believe what she built. A fuckin' robot! In high school! Can you believe it?'

I would blush and roll my eyes in the moment, nudging Dad to stop embarrassing me, and I would tell his friend not to listen to Dad's nonsense. 'You know how he exaggerates!' I would say. Inside, I was brimming, begging for him to go on.

To me, Dad didn't look like the other dads at these parties. He had a messily trimmed salt-and-pepper mustache from the seventies that rested above a perfectly straight set of white teeth with a small gap in the centre and below a large mushroom-like nose that bulged open whenever he was excited or angry. Dad had laser eye surgery to correct his far-sightedness by then but he still wore a pair of simple oval-shaped glasses that he'd misplace every couple weeks and which Mom would have to replace for a few bucks from the local pharmacy. Dad always wore a freshly ironed half-sleeved button-down shirt that sat loosely on top of his round belly. He usually kept his shirt un-tucked above a pair of egg-white slacks with a brown belt and recently shined black shoes.

Dad's hairline had started receding decades back, but he carefully maintained a few lonely strands of black and white hair that he'd comb down with love just before a party.

I felt a bittersweet aftershock in the car ride home from these parties, staring at the back of Dad's shiny head as he drove us home. It was the only time Dad told me how proud he was of me. Once home, Dad would yell at me to clean up my room and stop messing around and generally get my act together. I was never quite sure where I stood with him. He told his friends I was succeeding, but in private, he told me I was failing. Which was it? Could it be both?

'I came to this country with just a few dollars in my pocket. In Kenya, my brothers and I walked for miles just to get to school every day. Then I went to Manchester University, then UC Berkeley, while working at a gas station, got my master's, worked hard, got an entry job as an engineer, and now look at me. I was once rich for a few days when the markets were strong, you know? Look at your life; you have everything. Anything is possible if you work hard and stay on track,' Dad said.

Success was important to Dad. Success gave Dad a sense of belonging in the Silicon Valley Indian circles that he had to claw his way into.

Dad often chided me for having such a blatant disregard for money by telling me the story of his father immigrating to America to live the American Dream. When Grandpa came to America, he was a seasoned teacher, but all he could find was a menial job down the street pushing paper for meagre wages. I would picture my Dadaji, the man I saw as looming, quiet and always well put together with a fresh shave – a man who had raised eight children across four continents – begging a white man half his age for a job that was far below his skill set, all for the hope that America might change his children's and grandchildren's lives one day.

It was a scary thing to picture; a powerful story that fell on deaf ears at the time. I was a child of immigrant privilege born into a family that had acquired more than modest means in just one generation. The hardest challenge I overcame as a kid was wetting my bed. I had no concept of struggle whatsoever.

And yet, there was a time when I was fifteen years old, when I was so frustrated with my circumstances, so convinced I had been dealt a bad hand, that I locked myself in my room, threw open a bottle of stolen painkillers, and spread them across my bed and floor in meticulous disarray. Without ingesting a single pill, I turned up my Jewel cassette tape to the highest pitch on my boom box and I wailed and banged on the floor until my voice was raw. I desperately hoped my parents would find me and realize I needed more attention and love. Instead, my brother calmly unlocked my bedroom door with a straightened hairpin, found me curled up in the closet like a caged chipmunk, turned off my boom box, and told me that dinner was ready. ‘Come down when you’re done,’ Yogi said.

These were the tantrums and escapades of an upper-middle-income immigrant’s child in Fremont, California in the late 1990s.

It was clear what my purpose was to be in my father’s perspective: it was to get good grades so I could get a good education so that I would get a great job that would provide the family with pride and success. And because I was hell bent on making my father proud, I pursued his purpose with vigour and determination for many years.

I felt an incredible sense of worthiness, as if the clouds had parted and a light shone down on me, and only me, when Dad had something to brag about me. When I did well on a test, when I became the captain of the soccer team, when I was accepted into a well-known university, Dad would boast about me at a party, and like an obedient puppy being offered a treat, I would take it to my corner and lick my hands clean in delight.

Success, and the *appearance* of success, were Dad’s two driving motivators. I knew, ever since I was a kid, that success was important to Dad, and thus, important to me. I didn’t know what success actually meant to me, though I knew many definitions for failure.

The most painful of which at the time was, 'Look at Gopal and Amresh's kids! They all got into Stanford, Berkeley and MIT! In the EECS programs. So impressive. I wonder what we did wrong?'

Would I know I was a success once I beat all the other kids at everything? Would I know I was a success once we went to a party together and Dad bragged about me? Would it change when we got home? Could I call myself a success for more than an hour or two, some day? Would it always be momentary, or would it ever become final? When would I be allowed to call myself a success, full stop?

The emotional yo-yo kept me on my toes, and pushed me to accomplish what I have to this day. At the same time, it conflated and confused my motivations. Was I doing this because it would make Dad proud or because I believed in it? Was I doing it to prove to him I was as capable as anyone else out there, or because I cared about the work and the people I was creating my work for? Was I doing this because it was expected of me, or because it was what I expected of myself? How would I define my own success once I got there and Dad wasn't around to tell everyone about it?

In December of 2016 I wrote and publicly shared an article about one of the biggest failures in my life to date. Some of our friends and family read the piece and commented on it when they saw Dad at a party a few days later. Dad sent me a long email in response.

He wrote, 'You cannot make failure into some kind of skill set to share with the rest of the world. I have told you before and you have failed to hear me – there is nothing noble about failure. You reach nobility by learning from failure, and moving on. The universe is structured for us to fail. But we raise children, send them to great schools, expose them to challenges, so they will succeed and make the world a better place.'

I burned with shame. I had failed him once again.

Failures were to be hidden in our family; swept under the rug and burnt to ashes with us when we were cremated.

I knew what Dad meant by his email, though. Dad meant that he was scared for me. Dad wanted to protect me, keep me safe. While I leapt into the abyss with my eyes wide open and my arms outstretched, Dad wanted to hold me close and lull me to sleep with 'The Rime of the Ancient Mariner'.

My parents had given me everything I needed growing up: private schools, SAT tutoring, art classes, science clubs, Lego sets, soccer outfits and a trip around the world. Dad used to joke that I was born with a silver spoon in my mouth. As a kid, I would picture myself coming out of the womb and into the world, sucking on a tiny silver spoon with an ornate handle protruding from my lips.

The doctor would say, 'Ah yes, we've got another one with a silver spoon! How special!'

I felt like I had spent my whole life trying to spit that spoon out, while biting down hard on it at the exact same time. Dad's success was hard earned. My success was supposed to be inevitable.

◈

After weeks of my fear arguing with my alter ego while my cash reserves dwindled, in June of 2014, I wrote Dad and Mom a letter about the $24,000 loan I needed to build a business for parents and kids in India. Dad responded first, saying he would think about it.

I lapsed into a spiral of fear and doubt. What if he says no? Why did I have to ask him? Why does he need to think about it? Why doesn't he believe in me? Why doesn't he understand me? Will I always have to do exactly what he expects of me?

He sent me the money the following week with a letter of expectations for how the money should be spent and what I would have to do if this 'fun little project' wasn't working out within six months: find a normal job. It was fair, but it also hurt.

At the time, I felt relieved, nervous and frustrated. I felt like, finally, I could breathe for a few months, find an office space, find some teammates and pay their salaries while I searched for real, long-term investors in the company. But I also felt like Dad's money was weighted down with emotional debt. I felt like he would now have something on me. He had done me a huge favour, and I would now, and maybe forever, owe him.

Chapter 3

'The most important thing to do if you find yourself in a hole is to stop digging.'
—Warren Buffet

I spent the next three months networking, building the product, interviewing teammates, hiring and firing, and hiring again. One huge mistake I made early on was to hire someone who was an awful fit, both culturally and integrity-wise.

At the time, I was confident I could build a user-centred website, hire engineers, and take a great product to the 'market'– the market being parents. I had built basic websites before, either out of interest, for my own blog, or for my personal portfolio, and WordPress made the whole process one hundred times simpler. What I felt a lot less confident about was marketing and sales.

So, when I met a man who said he was an expert in digital marketing and search engine optimization (SEO) in August, who would work for almost nothing, I hired him. Two weeks later I noticed I was avoiding my new hire as much as possible. *My first hire*, I thought.

Most days, I would see him walking in and I'd sprint to the opposite end of our office with my laptop and pretend to take calls all day so that I wouldn't have to talk to him. We didn't enjoy spending time together, and we were the only two people in the company at the time.

Worse, he didn't know much about digital marketing or SEO at all. The initial pitch he had shown me when I interviewed him was stolen from someone else online, but I hadn't double-checked. I never imagined someone could be that audacious and immoral about their work. I had to get rid of him.

It was awful, though – it was the first time in my life I had to fire someone – and I went back and forth on my intuition for weeks. Sure, I had built two companies in the past, but somehow, I had escaped both without firing a single person. People always left on their own when it was clearly a bad fit or it got frustrating enough that they couldn't put up with me anymore. *Maybe that's part of why those businesses failed*, I wondered.

I called advisors and friends for their advice. I asked my boyfriend, Jonathan, what he thought I should do.

'Clearly, you need to rip the bandage off and get rid of this guy,' Jonathan bluntly said.

◈

Jonathan and I had met at the beginning of 2012 at the back of a now defunct jazz club in Mumbai called Blue Frog. We met at the bar when we both ordered our usuals – a gin and tonic with extra lime – and we exchanged business cards. He was building the education portfolio for a venture capital fund, Acumen, which I had admired and followed for years. I was selling cheap tablets to schools, which he thought was a colossal waste of time.

We had mutual friends who we danced and drank the night away with, before we all made our ways to our individual beds for the night.

Jonathan and I played cat and mouse for a year, chatting at educational conferences and meeting up for coffee, but never talking about our true feelings for each other.

We finally started dating at the beginning of 2013, when Jonathan wrote me a long letter about how he felt. To commemorate our relationship, we ran the Mumbai Half Marathon together. He ran his fastest time yet. I met him at the finish line half an hour later.

Maybe we'll always be playing a little bit of cat and mouse in our relationship, that way, I thought to myself.

◈

'It's not that simple,' I said to Jonathan. 'He's my first hire. What if I haven't given him enough of a chance to prove me wrong? What if I can't find anyone else who knows digital marketing? What if no one else will work for the pennies I'm paying him?'

Eyebrows raised, Jonathan stared back at me with a knowing look that said, 'Are you kidding?'

◈

I fired my first hire one month after hiring him. I spent the next month searching, interviewing, doubting, and poaching my next three employees in the company – Gajendra, Saif and Priyanka.

The four of us visited nearby schools to ask parents for their feedback when we put the first version of the product. I had hacked together this version with my basic web development skills. It went live on the Internet in October that year, in 2014. We called our company KleverKid – because 'Clever' was taken by another ed-tech company, and we wanted 'kid' to be in the title.

'Wow!' one parent said at a school in North Delhi. 'I've been looking for something like this to find classes for my child. How much does it cost?'

'It's free,' I told her. 'We charge the merchants a small fee, but it's totally free for you to browse and book!'

She was speechless.

My team and I went back to our Tetris-shaped, baby blue table in the back corner of someone else's startup office.

'We have something here, you guys,' Gajendra said.

'I think this is going to be big,' Saif said.

'I have so many ideas for how we can grow this!' Priyanka said.

Gajendra and Saif were two young men I had crossed paths with before KleverKid.

Gajendra, a Dhirubhai Ambani college graduate, had briefly interned for me in my first education technology startup, when I moved from Phnom Penh to Hyderabad in 2009, working with the professor from CMU, which we called Mobile and Immersive Learning for Literacy in Emerging Economies, or MILLEE. Gajendra was in his early twenties, tall and gangly like a basketball player, with eyes that turned soft and warm when he spoke to children. He had a dimpled face and a permanent five o'clock shadow with a thick head of hair that he would nervously fiddle with while he bounced his leg rapidly up and down, shaking the entire baby blue table we all worked on.

Gajendra had stayed committed to the cause of helping bring a better education to kids, even though he had since taken up a corporate job working for Airtel in his nine-to-five life. Gajendra, or 'GJ', as we nicknamed him, brought a sense of importance and seriousness to the work, much more so than anyone his age I had ever met. GJ deeply cared about the kids we served. I always wondered if his dogged commitment and willingness to take a huge pay cut stemmed from an effort to make up for a lost childhood of his own.

GJ was the guy I could rely on to get the work done at the quality and speed that I would have done myself. He had the work ethic of a mother squirrel scampering around at the end of fall, storing up food for the long winter to come. He was every entrepreneur's dream first-hire.

Saif, an entrepreneurial young marketing guru, had read about my work years before, ever since I moved to India in 2009, and began following my startup adventures through my blog and some talks I gave that were uploaded on YouTube. Saif, who was twenty-six-years-old, was short and stout with an endless reserve of energy. He decided to take the twenty-five-hour train ride from Hyderabad to Delhi for very little money and no guarantees of long-term employment whatsoever.

Saif was an idealist, a dreamer, and an artist. He could often be found at the office late into the evening playing with tiny plastic superhero figurines and creating a colourful installation dropping from the fan that loomed over our desk. Saif kept us all on our toes. He made us laugh and relax when we were anxious, hungry, worried and scared for our future as a company.

Priyanka and I met through a startup hiring and fundraising website called AngelList, where I had seen her profile and pinged her for a coffee.

Priyanka was initially only looking for a part-time business development role so that she could spend her free time on a handful of other entrepreneurial positions she held with other companies. She was tall like me, with an athletic build and long, wild hair that she'd twist into a bun with one flick of her wrist. We got along immediately, but I knew it would take a lot of convincing before she'd commit to KleverKid fulltime.

When I asked around about her, it seemed like every CEO in Delhi knew who Priyanka was. She had no ego about her skills, though. Priyanka was willing, excited even, to do the dirty work. Priyanka would wear any hat I gave her, she would try any new idea I threw at her, and she would complete her work with the kind of zeal you would typically find in a co-founder.

Priyanka, whom we abbreviated to 'PK', was sceptical upon first meeting me, which I respected about her.

'Isn't someone else doing something like this already?' she asked me.

'Yes, but it's crap and we're going to make something a hundred times better,' I said.

Many of the people I interviewed were Yes-Ma'am-men. They agreed with anything and everything I said, just to land the job. PK wasn't the type to encourage a fruitless idea or say yes out of blind respect.

In hindsight, I still believe these three hires were perfect for the stage we were at and the culture I wanted to build in this company. I think what I did wrong, though, was think of our startup as a 'family'. I called our team a family all the time, and while they didn't seem to be made uncomfortable by that, thinking of them that way made it that much more painful to withstand people quitting or, worse, having to fire them. It felt like a direct, personal insult – the way it might feel if a sibling or child were to desert their family. I must have read some famous CEO say that he treated his team like he would treat his family back then, but I took it too far. In hindsight, I think what he meant was that he treated his team with respect, rather than treating them like mules.

◈

After a month, all three of them, GJ, Saif and PK, were brimming over with pride and excitement for the crazy idea we were creating. They were each critical in our early days, and going forward, PK became my confidant, my Chief Operating Officer, and my go-to-person for every big decision we made in the company. Even the final one.

When I think back on those early days of the startup, I think it was both a dream and a nightmare. It was enrapturing; everything around us blurred into an almost-perfect harmony, and we lived inside the dream as if it might never end. But I was also more stressed out and anxious than I had ever been in my life. *How would I manage so many people? How would I pay their salaries? How would I not fail them, just like I had failed in the past?*

Then, as the end of October rolled around, I got an email from Dad. 'The six-month period you committed to is almost over, Shabnam. You agreed back in June to find a job by this point if things weren't working out. It seems like things are not working out yet. Please let me know your plan.'

Our account balance in the company had gone from $24,000 (Rs 14 lakh) to $2,000 (Rs 1.2 lakh) in what felt like one heartbeat. We would be broke soon, and I needed to find more money right away.

Chapter 4

'The biggest myth is that [startups] are fun.'
— Ben Horrowitz

I had never fundraised for any of my startups before. MILLEE, in 2009, had a huge donation come in from Nokia just before I joined the professor's team, so I could focus on growing the business back then, rather than searching for money. Perspectful, the consulting firm I had just shut shop on earlier in 2014 with the Californian co-founder, was an advisory consulting business for education companies, so it did not require venture capital at all. We simply started selling our advisory services to clients and paying ourselves whatever we could from the revenue we made.

This company, KleverKid, would need venture capital to work. I had done my research on online marketplaces, and I knew that most of them burnt a lot of money for many years before they became profitable. Ours would be no different.

Why would any smart investor invest in me, though?

I emailed, called, WhatsApp-ed, Facebook-messaged and LinkedIn-ed every single high-net-worth individual (HNI) and every entrepreneur I had ever met. The list was small, but I hit them from every desperate angle I could think of: Did they know any investors interested in education and parenting in India? Were they, themselves, interested in education and parenting in India? Would they be willing to make an introduction to someone who might be willing to make an introduction to someone who might be interested in education and parenting in India?

Perhaps they opened my message, skimmed it, and thought, 'Yikes, delete!' Maybe they read my WhatsApp and said to themselves, 'No, thanks.' I wonder if they gave it a second thought. I wonder if they heard the desperation in my words and said to themselves, 'Good luck, lady.'

A few of them did respond to me though. Of those who responded, 99 per cent said no. One, my old boss, Max, from 2011 when I briefly worked for Pearson, the largest education company in the world, said yes. He said he had moved on from Pearson, but he thought I should meet someone who might be able to help me out – probably not with money – but perhaps with some introductions. He said this person knew Mohandas Pai and K. Ganesh well.

Mohandas Pai was a director at Infosys and was considered the best chief financial officer in India. Not only that, but he also took a 'keen interest in improving literacy across the country, mainly primary education' and one of his investments 'aimed to feed 50,00,000 children by 2020,' as per Wikipedia. Meeting Mohandas Pai would be like meeting Bill Gates, I thought. What's his number? Can we call him now, I asked?

My ex-boss put his friend, Umashankar, on three-way call and we chatted for a while as I nervously paced around my barely-one-bedroom apartment late into the warm evening in October. I explained what I was trying to build with my team at KleverKid, and how much of a challenge it was to find investors who actually aligned with our vision and understood education deeply. Mohandas Pai understood education, I ventured. I wonder what he might think about this...?

Uma said he wanted to help, but to give him a few days to call around to some friends. He couldn't make any guarantees about 'Mohan,' as he called him, but he was sure someone would find this interesting, he said.

I let out a deep sigh that it felt like I had been holding in for months. Finally, someone who's on my side. Someone who understands what I'm doing. Someone who's rooting for me and can help me out. *Wait, why does this guy want to help me though?*

While I waited for Uma to get back to me, I got a response on LinkedIn from a different man who said he couldn't invest directly, but that he wanted to invite me to pitch my business at his conference in front of a panel of investors in Delhi in a few days.

Take the help you can get, I reminded myself.

I accepted, and prepared non-stop for hours upon hours, rehearsing my witty catchphrases and zingers to get everyone laughing, excited, and pulling out their chequebooks.

The man sent me another message while I was preparing, this time over WhatsApp, 'I like your profile picture,' he said, adding a wink emoji.

I wanted to say, that makes me feel uncomfortable, we have a business relationship, and it feels inappropriate for you to hit on me given the circumstances. But I didn't. That thought barely even registered at the time, and if I'm being honest, I thought that him liking my physical appearance might, somehow, give me a small leg up at the conference in a few days. Maybe he'd give me a better timeslot, maybe he'd introduce me in a more favourable way to the panel of investors. It sounds absurd when I think about it now, and sad and desperate, that I was willing to allow such an uncomfortable, awkward and inappropriate remark pass for the sake of a better timeslot. But I did.

And he knew I would. He knew he had power over me, and I needed him to let me pitch at his event. But when I think about it now, it makes my skin crawl. The number of times men in India used their position of power and money to say and do inappropriate things with me, I cannot even count anymore.

For a long time, as an entrepreneur, I saw myself as a pair of shoes that investors would walk in. Some investors, a select few, cherished their shoes. They only owned a few pairs, they shined them every morning, they walked around the puddles on the street when they could, and they put them away in the closet when they got home. Others couldn't care less about their shoes; they had hundreds of options for shoes to wear, they never had time to care for them, and they found it almost enjoyable to wear them down and take them through the harshest environments.

The truly sad part about this analogy is that I never believed that I was worthy of covering the former type of investor's feet. I believed those investors would never take me seriously, or that I needed to be a part of some exclusive club to get access to them. So, when I got access to a club, any club really, I jumped on the opportunity and told myself, just bite your tongue, pinch your nose and squint your eyes, everything will be okay once you find an investor.

Half an hour before the event started, I was rehearsing my pitch outside of the auditorium, when the organizer walked up to me and handed me a black short-sleeved, collared golf shirt with the event logo on it. 'Put this on,' he said.

A few thoughts went through my head right away.

One, this guy can't tell me what to wear! I thought. Who does he think he is?

Two, I thought about what might happen if I said no. *Will he throw me out of the event if I don't wear it?*

Three, I thought about how meticulous I was with my entire pitch. *I put so much time into finding the right outfit that made me feel confident, capable and smart enough to give this pitch in front of this huge audience. I can't change now; I'll lose my mojo.*

I was wearing a structured, bright magenta-coloured dress that day, and the black collared shirt he handed me felt, in that moment, like it would ruin everything. I was unravelling. I weighed my options, and ultimately, I decided that I'd rather be ejected from the pitch with some of my dignity intact than to give in to this man's whims once again.

'I'm sorry, but I can't,' I heard myself say to him.

He was stunned. People must have never said no to him. He started to yell at me about everything he had done to get me into this event and how ungrateful I was being. I told him I had worked hard and planned meticulously for this event. I told him I felt like his request was unreasonable and unprofessional at such a late stage in the process. We argued until a minute before I was supposed to get on stage, when he said I could either put the shirt on or leave.

I was desperate to raise a round of capital at this point having exhausted all the money Dad had lent me. I needed to find another way to pay my team's salaries, pay the office rent and grow my company. Soon, I wouldn't be able to pay the bills and everything would crumble to the ground.

I put the shirt on, and I walked out onto the stage.

As I got up on stage, everything in my brain went dark and cold. I fumbled along my presentation, stuttering and blabbering about irrelevant information. At one point, I accidentally cursed audibly into the microphone and caught one investor's eyes bulge, then strike something out on the paper in front of him.

When the clock ran out for my allotted pitch time, I was only halfway through what I had planned to say. Instead of putting the microphone down and earning a tiny bit of dignity back, I decided to pick up the pace and run rapid fire through the rest of the presentation.

The investor panel had to decide on the spot if they wanted to invest in the business or not, then announce their decision in front of the large audience, and on live television. I held my breath.

Investor 1 picked up the mic and said, 'I find this space very interesting – helping parents find classes for their kids sounds useful – but I have no idea how you'll make money, so I'll pass. Good luck.'

Investor 2 took the mic and said, 'I can tell you are very energetic and, uh, *passionate*, about this idea, but I am not sure you have the right team. I will not be able to invest. Sorry. Come back to me when you've got a stronger team!'

Investor 3 looked left and right and calmly stated, 'I have no idea how you're going to convince parents to use your product. It seems too far-fetched of an idea for me. I pass.'

Investor 4 said, 'I agree with the rest of the comments. Pass.'

Investor 5 looked sad. He said, 'You know, I was going to invest in this idea, but the other guys have convinced me not to. Sorry! Good luck.'

It felt like I was stuck buckled into the pilot seat of an airplane that had lost its propeller and was nose-diving straight into the ocean. I thought I couldn't breathe or move, but I felt my legs pull me off the stage and run my body out of the building and into the front seat of my car.

This event was supposed to change my life. Instead, I had failed miserably, and worse, publicly.

It wasn't until much later I realized how important this moment was for me; it was my first in a series of failures throughout KleverKid to first *define* what success meant to me, before chasing some mirage in the distance that everyone else said was 'success'. Sure, we needed money, fast, but was this the way I wanted to get it?

◈

After that first debacle with the marketing and SEO hire, I had become extremely particular about who I would hire to work for me; why wouldn't I apply the same scrutiny to who I would take on as an investor? Why would I leave it up to the random chance that someone, anyone, might be convinced within five minutes of stage time and say yes? And if they had, I would have no choice but to accept. It would be disrespectful and self-sabotaging to reject an offer like that, regardless of what the terms were. We've all seen Shark Tank, right?

I cried in my car for a few minutes, or maybe it was hours, gave myself a little pep talk to hold it together, turned my ignition on and drove home, wondering how I could ever leave my house again, or how I'd face my teammates without feeling the heat of humiliation, shame and failure. I considered calling Dad for advice, but decided to delay it until I had processed what just happened, and could somehow spin it so I wouldn't have to hear the same response, 'You need to find a normal job, find something stable.'

When I took a step back and considered what the investors said to me on stage that day, I could tell *something* might be brutally wrong about my business, but it wasn't obvious to me at the time exactly what it was. The fear in my head got the best of me, and took over my rational thinking.

Was it my pitch style? Was it the photo on our homepage? Was it our number of retweets per day? Was it my team? Was it my product? Was it our geography? Was it my market? Was it the investors I was talking to? Was it just me?

I was not entirely sure any of these investors were the right investors for me – we weren't told beforehand who would be sitting on that panel, but when I researched their portfolios later, none of them had invested in the education, kids or parenting markets. So, why take their feedback to heart? My alter ego tried to silence the fear in my head, 'They can fuck off,' she said.

A couple days later, on a Tuesday, Uma called me back with good news. He had lined up a meeting with the eminent Mohandas Pai for me. I should book a flight to Bangalore for Wednesday.

'Tomorrow?' I confirmed.

'Yes, tomorrow! A slot opened for him last minute. You should take advantage,' Uma said. 'This is a once in a lifetime opportunity.'

'I know, it's just very soon. I have no time to prepare,' I said, pacing in my apartment, hearing my alter ego and my fear argue loudly with one another. *She's not ready. She is ready, she just needs to suck it up and take the meeting. She needs more time. There's no time to think, she needs to believe in herself, she's ready!*

'Hello? Are you there?'

'Yes, I'm here Uma. Sorry. Okay, I will book my flights and meet with him tomorrow.'

'Great! I will send over the details right away. Good luck!'

'Thanks.'

'Oh, one last thing. What were you planning to wear when you meet him?'

'Wear? I'm not sure…why?'

'Well, you know, Mohan is a bit of a conservative man, and I know you like to wear…um…*American* dresses…I think it might be better if you wore an Indian kurta tomorrow.'

One beat. Two beats. *What the fuck? Who is this guy? Is this literally the second time I'm being told what to wear in one week? Where am I?*

'Oh, that's interesting. Thanks for letting me know,' I said.

'Alright, good luck tomorrow. Call me afterwards!'

Click.

I stared at myself in the mirror. Was I putting investors off so much by what I wore that they felt compelled to tell me how to dress for a formal business meeting? I had never worn a kurta to a business meeting; on me, kurtas felt ill fitting, informal and unstructured. A structured, knee-length business dress with high heels was my go-to power outfit. It made me feel like Superwoman.

Doing things my way didn't seem to be working for me, though. This meeting with Mohan was my one shot, and Uma had known him for decades. *Maybe now is not the time to be righteous and feminist, I thought. Perception matters, more than my capabilities, I guess. Might as well go for broke and take the advice,* I said to myself.

I opened my closet and dug around the back-corner pile that had started gathering dust. All the clothes I never wore sat back there. I found a bright orange kurta that was made in chikankari stitching, originating from Lucknow, near my mother's hometown. At the least, I thought, I can summon Mom's strength, if I can't summon Superwoman's. She's pretty close.

I slowly ironed the kurta out with my laptop opened to my pitch deck on the other end of the ironing board. I mumbled my script to myself, pausing for nods here, waiting for laughter there.

This would be a one-on-one meeting, so I'd have to change my pitch a bit. Make it more personal. Mohandas Pai also knew a lot about education, so there was that to consider – I didn't need to educate him about how schools were not doing enough to help kids find their passion. He would know that already.

I laid my kurta out on the couch with a pair of slacks and flats. I got into bed but I couldn't sleep. There was no point trying; my flight from Delhi to Bangalore was at 5.25 a.m.

I got out of bed at 2 a.m., showered, washed my hair and pinned it back in a bun. I didn't put any makeup on. I'll show him conservative, I thought. I slipped into my orange kurta and my black slacks and knelt to put my flats on. I noticed they were torn near the toes. When I lifted my hands, they were shaking. I tried to steady them by holding them together in prayer.

Namaste. The spirit within my Fear bows to the spirit within my Alter Ego. It's go time.

I unplugged my laptop and checked my watch. It was 2.30 a.m. Might as well wait at the airport, I thought.

I called a cab and closed my eyes in the backseat for the twenty-minute ride. At least there's no traffic in Delhi at 2.30 a.m. I checked in for my flight and sat down at my gate. I checked my watch. It was 3 a.m.

By 5.00 a.m., my stomach was starting to ache from anxiety. I was on my fourth cup of coffee since I had arrived at the airport, and my flight was finally boarding. It was IndiGo.

I remembered meeting the president of IndiGo at a social enterprise conference in 2012 in Hyderabad.

Aditya was young, with a shiny bald head, and stylish square glasses. He talked about how IndiGo's goal was not to build what customers wanted, but what customers were willing to pay for – cheap flights that were on time and hassle-free, which was unheard of at the time. I remembered he wore a blue t-shirt to speak to a large audience that day. Not a suit.

I looked down at my bright orange kurta and breathed a deep sigh. *My clothes do not define me*, I said. I took my seat on the plane and fell asleep for three hours.

When I arrived in Bangalore at 8.30 a.m., I hailed a cab to Mohandas Pai's office. But I was early. Very early – my meeting was at 11a.m. I was so early that the office was not even open yet, so I walked down the street to find a place for coffee and breakfast. There was a large local dosa shop just across the street from his office, but when I sat down, I realized Kannada was the operative language. My Hindi would do me no good here. When the waiter arrived, with desperate, begging eyes, I pointed to someone else's meal and said, 'Please,' with folded hands. He nodded and left.

I opened my laptop and rehearsed to myself. 'Product-market fit, go-to-market plan, exponential marketplace growth, exceptional team, change children's lives in India, democratize learning.'

My hands were shaking again. I laid my left hand flat on the table and stretched my fingers out as far apart as I could stretch them.

When we were kids, my brother and I used to play a game when we went to restaurants. We'd hold a sharp knife in one hand and compete to see how quickly we could stab the table with the knife between the outstretched fingers of the other hand on the table, jumping from the space between two fingers to the next. We had seen a magician do it on a TV show one time. Yogi would inevitably win, and I would accuse him of cheating. We were always competing that way, trying to one-up each other and make Mom and Dad proud. *I wonder what he would say if he could see me now*, I thought.

My dosa came and I scarfed it down in seconds.

I asked the waiter for the check and when I put my credit card on the table he shook his finger in my face. Cash only. I waived the card, and showed him my empty wallet, *no cash*, I motioned. He shrugged and walked away. I dug in my giant purse for change – the bill was less than 100 rupees – and pulled out, in coins, the exact change to match the bill. *Sorry, buddy, no tip for you.* I ducked out of the restaurant before he could run after me.

When I took the elevator up to the third floor of Mohandas Pai's office, I held my breath. *This is it. Gotta give it everything you've got.*

The secretary told me I'd have to wait, 'Sir is in another meeting,' she said.

I sat in the front foyer for half an hour, rubbing my hands against my pants to dry the beads of sweat that formed every two minutes. Finally, the secretary told me I could go in.

As I walked into Mohandas Pai's office, I noticed two things: his TV was playing the news, loudly, and his office was a mess with stacks of paper everywhere. He asked me to come in and sit down.

Growing up in America, I hadn't learned the foundational culture expectations and custom traditions that were standard when it came to formal business meetings in India. In India, you addressed everyone older than you or who was considered professionally above you with 'Sir' and 'Maam'. In India, it was antiquated to use the hand gesture of Namaste to greet elders, although I still did with my relatives in America. In India, you waited at the door for the teacher to let you into her classroom, just as you would at someone's office. 'May I come in?' you'd say.

I walked in and sat down.

T.V. Mohandas Pai was a big guy. Not only had he accomplished an immense amount of work – he was the CFO at Infosys, India's largest IT consulting firm, for over a decade, and then took over Manipal Education Group, one of the most notorious higher education institutions in India – but he was literally, physically a big man. He had a chubby face with one thick eyebrow and one thin, and a speckling of white in his beard that made him look friendly, like an Indian Santa Clause.

When he looked directly at me, though, it felt like he could see right through me. I swallowed hard. I knew I should call him Sir, but after five years of living in India, it still felt awkward and uncomfortable to me. *Let him start.*

'So, Uma tells me good things about you. How can I help?' he said with his eyes fixed back on the TV to my right. He had a deep voice that shook my chair.

'Well, I'm building a startup in education and parenting, and Uma thought you might be the right person to chat with,' I said, wringing my hands to stop them from shaking.

'What does the business do?'

'It helps parents find the best afterschool activities for their kids.'

'How do you make money?'

'We don't make any money yet, Mohan Sir, but we plan to make money through bookings. We'll list the merchant programmes for free but charge them a small per cent for every student that books a seat through us. Like ClassPass and AirBnB, but for children.'

'The gym and hotel industry is very different from the education industry, though. How will you get parents to your site?'

'We have a go-to-market plan, with content marketing, referral fees, and Mommy meet-ups.'

'Tell me, why are you doing this? For the money or the impact?'

One beat. Two beats. Three beats.

'That's a good question,' I said to Mohandas Pai. 'To be honest, I'm not sure which is more important to me. I have always believed you should only do work that makes a positive impact on the world and you cannot make an impact without finding a way to financially sustain the work you do, so they go hand in hand, in my mind.'

'If you had to pick?'

'I would pick the kids, the impact.'

'Hmm, I see. You know, running a startup is hard work. Many fail. How do you know you will survive?'

I thought back to the first business I ever tried to build, in college in 2005.

◈

In November 2005, an earthquake had devastated Kashmir; a place I could barely identify on a map. Eighty-seven thousand three hundred and fifty people were reported dead, nineteen thousand of them children, three million five hundred people were made homeless. At nineteen-years-old, with blurry eyes and a raging hangover, I read the news from my dorm room in Pittsburgh. Wrapped up in a comforter in her bed across the room from mine, my Pakistani roommate, Mehvish, snored softly into the cold hours of the morning light.

While I read the news, I thought about Mom. Mom often told me stories of her childhood growing up in

India. Mom grew up in a small town in the northern part of India called Sangrur. One night, she told me about how, when she was my age, she washed her only salwaar kameez by hand every day before she went to bed, so it would be clean to wear to school the next day. Mom told me about the following summer, when she and her sisters borrowed the school textbooks from their classmates so they could copy the textbook word for word, by hand, and use that, instead of a real textbook, over the school year. I listened to her story from the safety of my bed and with my eyes squeezed shut, I tried to picture what her life must have been like before she married Dad and came to America. Mom's life always seemed so far away from mine, so improbable. It felt like her life could have gone two ways, and she lucked out.

As I continued reading the news, I realized I knew very little about the conflict between Pakistan and India over the land of Kashmir at the time. What I did know, is that Dad said he would disown me if I ever considered marrying a Pakistani man. While I looked, and spoke, and danced, and ate just like my Pakistani roommate, we were from opposite sides of enemy lines and Kashmir stood in contention between us. This earthquake did not care about country lines or religions, though, and neither did I.

I could still remember the HEX number for the hue of yellow Sean, Alicia and I used in the card, later that month.

I remembered the radius of the bevelled edges we made so that the card would feel different from a business card, but not exactly like a credit card either. I remembered the font we created to look like the Pittsburgh Steeler's logo, but not the same either. I remembered the moment, the euphoria, of realizing we could play on the word 'stealer'. We were so clever.

Sean and I had known each other from a distance in high school. He was a year younger than me. Sean was shorter than me, too, with heavily jelled into place brown hair, a square jaw, a huge nose, and big floppy ears framing his small face. Alicia was in design school at Carnegie Mellon, and in one of the Architecture classes that I took behind Dad's back. Analog Chip Design 3045 in my fated Engineering program did not quite stoke my creative fire. Alicia had long brown hair, a silver nose ring pierced into the left side of her nose and eyes the colour of the sea.

Alicia offered to help Sean and I design the cards that we would sell to students at Carnegie Mellon and the University of Pittsburgh. These cards, for a small fee of $5, would give students discounts to neighbouring cafes, flower shops, bookstores and restaurants. All the profits we made would go to rescuing children from the earthquake in Kashmir.

This was before Groupon or Yelp existed, but long after cutting coupons had gone out of fashion. Undergrads were notoriously cheap patrons, even the ones who attended college at expensive, private universities like CMU. That made it easy to lure them out of their dorm rooms for the sake of a discount.

When Sean and I approached local shops about our new business opportunity, we assumed it would be an easy sell: the small business owner would get more long-term customers for a small initial discount. We set our sights high – we were going to close on Subway too. Reality proved a bit more difficult though.

Many of the stores we approached were franchises, and could not offer discounts without higher-up approval. A no-go. The local mom-and-pops shops were operating on such slim margins, they fought with us to bring the discount down to tiny, meaningless percentages that wouldn't help students much. Not only that, they demanded long drawn-out contracts that stipulated every possible scenario, like the off-chance a tornado hit their only store and fifty students showed up the next day to claim their 2 per cent discount off a coffee.

Sean and I powered through. We were determined to make this idea work, and launch a successful business that could 'do well by doing good,' a phrase we had heard Bill Gates use in a speech he gave at CMU once. After knocking on doors, finalizing deals, signing on the dotted lines and delivering copies of contracts to twenty shops, we got the cards designed with Alicia, and we went to press printing thousands of cards out. We even got a write up in the Carnegie Mellon paper about us.

'Discounts and deals on top of charity? It doesn't get much better than this...Sophomore Sean J. Weinstock and junior Shabnam Aggarwal think they've got it. At a mere $5 per student, the Bargain Steeler Card offers discounts at local food shops ranging from Papa John's to Ben and Jerry's Ice Cream. The best part is that proceeds go to disaster relief efforts. The ultimate goal is to raise $10,000.' It was a win-win and our names were in print. Sean and I sent the article to our parents.

It was our first day of sales and we were ready. Everything was set up on a sign-up table in prime location for foot traffic in the middle of CMU's campus. Our first customer walked directly over to our table, as if on a mission.

'Are you selling the Bargain Steeler Card here?' she asked.

'Yes!' I said. Tears filled my eyes. Our first sale, I thought.

'Someone in the president's office wants to see you,' she said.

'Wow! Okay! One second,' I said. Sean and I locked eyes, thirsty for recognition. 'Sean, you stay here and sell, I'll go,' I said.

I followed her down the hallway and into the office I had passed a thousand times on my way to class, but had never entered. A forlorn old woman looked up from her desk at me as I entered.

'You're Shaubnaum?' she said. She pronounced my name with the long, drawn out a that I had come to accept from Americans. Sometimes, I even introduced myself to Americans that way, just to make things easier.

I nodded. My eyebrows were raised as high as my hairline and my mouth spread wide with anticipation. This would be what I had waited my whole life for. This would be the loving pat on the back, the Rocky-style raising of my fist as winner on the top podium, from a person of authority, at an institution that my father respected. This would be my shining moment. I had worked hard. I had accomplished something difficult. I had finally done it. I was going to be named a success.

'Please sit down. Can I see the card you're selling?'

I handed her the card in my hand, fingering the round edges and admiring the colour of mustard yellow under the harsh, white-tube lighting.

'Unfortunately, I can't let you sell this card. We risk being sued by the Pittsburgh Steelers Football team since you've used their trademarked name in your logo,' she said.

My eyebrows dropped. My smile replaced with wide faced horror.

'But...we are about to start selling them in the next five minutes,' I stammered. 'We've printed thousands of cards. We've already got pre-sales and donations made out to starving kids in Kashmir!'

I spiralled.

'I'm sorry. There's nothing I can do; this came from Legal. I can't let you sell this card to our students,' she said.

My first thought, in that moment, sitting on the hard, wooden chair in the administrator's office hearing I had to shut down what hadn't even truly begun yet, was not about the CMU students whose money I'd have to return out of my own pocket. It was not about the children in Kashmir who would no longer receive our ongoing support. It was not about Alicia who had helped us design the card, and to whom I could no longer offer any compensation. It was not even about Sean, my co-founder, who was sitting outside in the freezing cold setting up individual sign-up forms with Bic pens at the sales table.

My first thought was Dad. What would I tell him? How would he react? Would he be disappointed in me?

In that moment, much of my rational thought clouded, as if lightning was about to strike, I ran for shelter in the one place I feared judgement from most. I called my dad.

'Dad, it's me,' I said, sobbing.

'What's up, kiddo?'

'They won't let us sell the cards. They shut us down.'

'What happened?'

'The legal team said we couldn't use the Steeler's name, some issue with being sued.'

'Oh. I told you to stop messing around and focus on your school. How are your grades in Analog Design?'

I paused, lost. Alone.

'My grades are fine, Dad. I gotta go.'

I couldn't believe he was asking me about my grades at a time like this. I needed my father to tell me that I had tried hard, that I had done the right thing, and that it wasn't my fault it didn't work out. I needed him to tell me I was good and he was proud. I needed him to take my burden off my shoulders so I could breathe again. Instead, he pretended like it didn't happen. It was a different path, a tangent, and he wanted no part in it.

I went back to the table and told Sean to shut it down. We talked about changing the name, fighting the Legal team, finding another way. We were tired and frustrated. Things hadn't gone our way for the first time in our lives, and nothing would change that. However minor the implications, we had failed.

◈

'There's no way to know,' I said to Mohandas Pai. 'We could fail, but I am confident I will never give up on this mission.'

'Alright, well, let me see what I can do. Keep me in the loop on this – send me the numbers and your goals for the quarter. Let's talk soon.'

'Thank you, sir. I appreciate your time.'

◈

I walked out of Mohandas Pai's office ten minutes after walking in. In a daze, I walked down the hall, down the stairwell, out to the street, and waited. I waited for everything to sink in. I waited to comprehend what just happened. Was he going to invest? He didn't say. I didn't ask. I forgot to talk about my team, my product, my credentials. What happens now? Did I fly to Bangalore just for that?

I called Uma.

'Sounds like it went okay. Let me talk to him. I'll make some more introductions, just in case.' Uma said.

I was the kind of entrepreneur that put all her hopes on every single meeting with every single investor. Each meeting felt like a tiny opportunity for validation from a man my father's age. Last week, five men my father's age had told me I was not good enough. The month before, seventeen others had said the same. Today, another man was telling me...what? That I might be good enough? That he wants to stay in touch? What did that mean?

I called PK.

'How are things over there?' I asked her.

'Things are good. How did it go with Mr Pai?'

'It went fine. I'm not sure. It was a little odd.'

'Hmm, okay. I'm sure it went well. Don't worry so much. When are you back in Delhi?'

'Tonight,' I said. 'I'll explain more at the office tomorrow. Sleep with your fingers crossed.'

Click.

Next, I called my accountant, Ravi, who was quickly becoming the closest thing I had to a CFO, but was only consulting part-time for me. A mutual friend in Bombay had introduced us, and he was the first honest accountant I had ever talked to. He knew what he didn't know, and I liked that about him.

'How many weeks do we have left?' I asked Ravi.

'Shabnam, we can barely pay salaries and rent this month. We don't have much left.'

'Can we make it to December?' I pleaded. 'I don't think I'll be able to close any new funding until then.'

'Yea, I think I can stretch it that far, but it's going to be tough. We'll have to delay some payments. I can delay my own consulting fees for a bit.'

'Okay, thanks Ravi. I believe in you! Make it happen. You're the best. Call you later.'

Click.

I took a few more meetings in Bangalore stuck in a daze that day. I was too exhausted to process anything else. Was every investor meeting going to be like this, I thought to myself. Would I have to dress this way for each of them? Would any of them tell me directly, yes or no? Was I going to have to guess at the meaning of their words with all of them? How long could I keep this up before going mad?

I knew I needed to line up a lot more meetings like this one in November if I planned to close a round by December. Jeff Bezos said he got one hundred noes before he got his first yes. I was already clocking twenty-two noes with the email and LinkedIn rejections as well as that debacle on stage. This one with Mohandas felt like a maybe, but everything I knew about maybes was that they were noes shrouded behind pig's lipstick.

At the time, I was not willing to accept a pseudo no, though. He told me to keep in touch, and I'd planned to do exactly that.

Chapter 5

'Running a startup is like chewing glass and staring into the abyss. After a while, you stop staring, but the glass chewing never ends.' – Elon Musk

I celebrated Diwali the next day, 23 October, quietly and by myself at home in my apartment in Safdarjung Enclave. I lit a few candles in the doorways, just in case Lakshmi happened to pass by and wanted to bestow me with some prosperity. I sat down on my couch with Ben Horrowitz's *The Hard Thing About Hard Things* and a large glass of golden whiskey with two cubes of ice. The apple doesn't fall that far from the tree.

I thought about family – Mom and Dad were visiting India soon, in November, for my cousin's wedding in Punjab. Jonathan, who had recently quit his job running the education portfolio at Acumen Fund in Mumbai, was moving to Delhi so we could live together after long-distance dating for a year and a half. It all felt like it was happening so fast and yet, I felt like I had no control on any of it whatsoever. I had to find a path forward that would allow me to build this startup and live my life with some sanity. I had to find funding right away.

I spent November getting more rejections. It would be more accurate to say that I spent November getting maybes, and maybe laters, and maybe when things change in this way or that. With all my noes and maybes, I was nearing fifty rejections.

In one meeting at one of his first offices in Gurgaon, the founder and CEO of Zomato, Deepinder, said to me, 'The climate for funding is changing in India. You're not going to have an easy time finding venture capital for this idea like you would have had in 2012 and 2013. Investors in India are a little bit behind those in Silicon Valley, but Indian investors are becoming savvier too, and they will not be quick to jump into investing in a marketplace idea like yours in 2014. It's a very difficult product to sustain.' He had just raised $60 million.

'Why don't you think about starting a school, instead?' he asked. 'I could find some friends who would invest a little bit in a school with me.'

I nodded my head with a tight-lipped smile, faking appreciation, so as not to offend a man that had power in this world. A man that could black-ball me with all Indian VCs with just one email. I shook his hand, thanked him for his support, and watched him walk away from me under the bright florescent lights past rows and rows of people staring at their laptops.

I slammed the door on the way out and gave his wannabe-Yelp company the middle finger. At least my marketplace was novel, different and helping kids, I thought. You go start a school.

He wasn't wrong, though. The climate was changing, and within a year, I would see exactly what he meant. Worse, he was right that I didn't know the first thing about building a marketplace product.

Marketplaces require large amounts of extremely patient venture capital before they're able to sustain on their own. They don't turn a profit overnight like a successful business to consumer (B2C) or business to business (B2B) startup would. Marketplaces are B2B2C, so you must build up *both sides* of the market at the same time – much like a flea market. At a flea market, if you, as the organizer, have only convinced sellers to come and sell their goods, but you haven't got enough buyers, it'll be a flop – sellers would be frustrated and never come back. Similarly, if you've convinced buyers with great advertising and marketing to come buy from your flea market, but the sellers don't show up, it'll still be a flop with frustrated buyers who will never come back. So, you must convince both sellers and buyers to come at the same time, and buy and sell similar things, and hope that you'll turn a small profit by being the middleman. Ten years after starting up Zomato with $444 million in investments, Zomato still spends more money than it makes today; they're still not profitable (but they claim to have positive unit economics).

◈

Luckily, Mohandas Pai meant what he said. I incessantly followed up with him after our meeting, sending him the user growth numbers and giving him updates, and one day, in the middle of December, he finally put me in touch with his fund manager, Deepak.

By then, Jonathan had moved in with me. Mom and Dad visited India the same week Jonathan had moved in. Sometimes I think I was intentionally, masochistically trying to make life harder for myself for no clear reason.

Jonathan was the first boyfriend I'd ever decided to 'live in sin' with. I knew my parent's stance on this – they may have brought me up in America, let me befriend the Caucasian girl down the street who taught me swear words and explained that kissing couldn't make me pregnant, they even allowed me to wear spaghetti strap shirts with blue glitter eye shadow to school – but living with a man before marriage was a little too liberal even for them.

I nervously paced the apartment moving Jonathan's boxes from one corner to the other, wondering how Mom and Dad would react.

I was twenty-nine years old, an entrepreneur with the CEO title on my business cards, I hadn't lived with my parents since I was eighteen, and yet, I was still desperate for their approval. I was still holding on to their judgement like a grown adult clutching her baby blanket. I had been living off their money for the last six months, though, and I knew that we were all very aware of that fact. That fact gave them my dependency, and my dependency meant they had a say.

By this point in my life, my parents and I had come to somewhat of a gentleman's agreement about my life decisions: they would make their opinion heard, often multiple times, but they seemed to recognize I was highly unlikely to change my decisions. We agreed that I should be aware of their dismay, at the least.

It didn't take long for Dad to make his opinion heard on Jonathan moving in, 'This isn't right, you know? This isn't who we are. Maybe if you were engaged it would be a different story. Our family doesn't live like this, Shabnam.' He only used my full name when he was really upset.

'I know Dad, I'm sorry. We love each other, but I'm not going to make a commitment that's lifelong until I know we can put up with each other day in and day out. I'm not easy to deal with, you know?'

Mom was quietly making chai in the kitchen. Jonathan had left for a meeting.

'That's beside the point. What will people think? What will I tell Prem and Asha if they ask me about you? How can you go against our family values like this?'

'I honestly don't understand what the big difference is. If we were living apart we'd just be spending more money and staying over at each other's places all the time. This is just practically and financially smarter.'

'Do you need money? I'll give you more money if that's what you need.'

'No, Dad, that's not the point. This is just how relationships work now, you know? It's different from your time.'

'In my time, we barely even met each other before marrying, this is obviously very different. I'm no idiot, Shabnam. Do you think I'm living under a rock?'

'Dad…'

'You know, so many of your friends are already married and even having kids. Why don't you stop all this nonsense and start a family if you like kids so much?'

'I will Dad, someday.'

'Not someday, today! Madhu, what do you think? Don't you have anything to say about all this?'

'Leave me out of this,' Mom said. 'She can do whatever she wants, she's not a child anymore. It's not like she's going to listen to you, anyway.'

'Mom, that's not fair. I listen to you guys; just because I don't do what you want me to do doesn't mean that I'm not listening.'

'What's the point of listening if you don't change your behaviour?' Dad said.

Sometimes it could go back and forth like this for hours between us, but on this day, I've had enough.

Dad was, and perhaps will always be, my biggest fan and my harshest critic. When he was proud of me, I knew I had done a good job. When he was mad at me, I felt ashamed and frustrated and sad, but by this point, I also started to wonder if his anger was a signal that I was doing something right.

Dad's anger told me I was not following the path he set out for me, and more and more, I was beginning to see that as a positive rather than a negative.

I *wanted* to be different. I wanted to be the black swan, the ugly duckling. I wanted to stand up and stand out and figure out what the best version of myself could be. I didn't want to follow the rules or fit into any box just because it was safe, or worse, just because people would feel more comfortable and proud of me.

Wasn't that sort of the point of prosperity?

At the top of Maslow's Hierarchy of Needs was Self-Actualization.

I knew I had a long way to go still, but I was beginning to see two clear paths forward for myself; one that Dad stood ahead of me on that was safe, comfortable, and straight, and one that my alter ego stood ahead on that was curved, complex and scary. The only question was, if I stayed on the latter path and ended up far away from the straight one, would Dad still love me? Would my family still care about me? Would I still belong somewhere?

◈

I emailed Deepak constantly after we were introduced by Mohan in December. Deepak said he had been out of town but KleverKid was an interesting idea, to send him the deck and give him some time to think through the details. I should also line up some co-investors in the meantime, he said, to de-risk and diversify my investor pool. He would send over a term sheet soon.

This was a huge windfall. This meant that Mohandas Pai might lead my first venture capital round, meaning he would put the terms down and he would take a board seat, in my first round of funding at KleverKid. This was the kind of ideal first funder that every entrepreneur prays for; well known, respected and knowledgeable.

But there were no guarantees yet. A term sheet is not a legally binding agreement, it simply tells you what the investor's offer would be, if they were to invest in your company, and I had no idea who, if anyone, would co-invest either.

I reached back out to exactly the same people I had reached out to before over LinkedIn, Facebook, WhatsApp and email, but this time, I name dropped. Mohandas Pai was planning to lead the round, I said, would you be interested in joining now?

Yes. Yes. Yes.

I had never heard so many yeses before. It was unbelievable; the sheer power of a name. Everyone wanted to get in the door, and I let them come in. By the middle of January, I had eleven other small investors interested in the round, including both of Mohandas Pai's sons, Pranav and Siddharth.

Things were starting to turn around, finally.

◈

But the team sitting around the baby blue Tetris shaped desk working on their broken laptops was not doing so well. Ravi and I were barely able to scrape together salaries in December, and there was no way I'd have the cash to pay salaries in January. The end of the month was approaching fast. I kept telling the team that we had interest, investors were close to closing a large round of venture capital with us, and the team could feel the excitement, but they also needed to pay their bills.

Not only that, but my team's hands were tied without any money to try innovative things at the company. PK wanted to try inviting local moms to kitty parties where she could advertise KleverKid and increase word of mouth referrals. GJ wanted to find a way to automate listing new merchants on the website. Saif wanted to hire an SEO consultant to get KleverKid on the top of the first page of Google searches for 'best programs for kids'. I wanted to rebuild the website. It would all cost money that we didn't have.

As a small, young startup team, we knew we had to make sacrifices, but by this point, everyone was living hand to mouth, and without one pay cheque they'd risk getting kicked out of their apartments or being unable to buy their own lunch.

At this point, I became doubly desperate to close the investment round. I could not bear the idea that these three people had given up everything else in their lives, and convinced their worried parents that they should leave stable, well-paying jobs, to come work with me, and now I couldn't even pay them enough to cover their rent.

By the end of January, Deepak had sent me the term sheet, we had gone back and forth over major and minor terms that made my head spin, along with my having to convince eleven other investors that these were favourable terms for them as well. Two of the smaller investors dropped out in the process, but it was okay because we still had nine investors plus Mohandas Pai, totalling the first round of 'seed' capital to $235,000 with a pre-money valuation of $1 million. I had apparently created a company worth 1 million dollars.

The legal work for the investment round would begin as soon as we finished our negotiations. My team and I celebrated by yelping and hugging and drinking Kingfisher on the balcony of someone else's office until the late hours of the night. I cried from exhaustion. I let out a deep sigh.

But, still no final agreement, and no actual money in the bank yet.

If I could go back, I would have planned for this. Fundraising is a six-month process from start to finish, at minimum, and that's only if you're lucky. Sometimes, it can take over a year. There's the first conversation, then follow up conversations, the financial evaluation, the term sheet, the negotiations, the legal work, more legal work, and then, finally, if all goes well, the money hits the bank. By the time I had my first conversation with Mohan in October of 2014, I had barely two months of cash left in the bank, and I had no prospects for significant revenue anytime soon. It was foolish and naive to think I would get money in the bank within two months.

With sorrow and pain, I approached my team's desk in late January of 2015. It was a gloomy overcast day in

January, still cold and damp in the far corner of the office we shared, and we had just finished celebrating our huge and unexpected fundraising success.

'I need to talk to you guys,' I said.

'What's up?' GJ said.

Pause. Deep breath.

'I need more time to pay your January salaries,' I said.

Pause. Wait.

'Oh, okay. That's okay, Shab,' Saif said. 'Don't worry. We'll figure something out.'

'Yea, it's fine. We will survive. Don't stress, Shab,' PK said.

I couldn't believe their reaction. It was the most humbling moment in my life. The sacrifice these three people – who didn't even know me that well – were willing to make for the sake of a crazy idea I had to 'democratize learning' was weighed on me immensely. *Why were they doing this for me? Why did they believe in me? What if I couldn't make it happen? What if I let them down?*

'When do you think the money will come in?' GJ said.

'I'm hoping next month. It's hard to say. I'm so sorry about this. I know it's unfair and puts you all in a tough position. But I promise I will figure something out by February end.'

I promised myself that day that I would never force my team to go a month without salary again, or to have to be the ones to make their CEO feel like it was okay to not pay them. It felt wrong, like I had sold them magic beans that didn't work and I had run away with their hard-earned money.

The actual investment capital in KleverKid wouldn't hit our bank account until 1 May 2017. In the meantime, I would beg, borrow, or steal from anyone I could, other than my team and my parents, to pay their salaries. I once even considered selling the Tag Heuer watch my parents gave me as a graduation gift when I graduated from CMU in 2007, but it wouldn't be enough.

By the end of February, I convinced Deepak to loan me a personal advance on Aarin's, Mohandas Pai's fund, investment capital so that I could loan that money out to KleverKid and KleverKid could pay everyone's salaries out. This was an easy way to get access to the money we were due, but prior to completing all the paperwork which could, and did, take months.

My relationship with Deepak was becoming more complex and strained by the day though, and in hindsight, any one of the ten or fifteen times we strongly disagreed in those early days should have been a clear indicator to me that this was not a great fit for either of us.

Jonathan was becoming more and more frustrated with the situation as well. Jonathan had been an investor with Acumen for years, so having him on my side, giving me advice throughout this process was invaluable. The only problem was that Jonathan was one of those investors who truly cared about each pair of 'shoes' he owned. He researched, he compared, he took his time, and once he decided to buy, he was careful with them. He polished, shined, and cared for every pair of shoes he had. He only owned a few pairs as an investor, and he wanted to own them for a long time.

Deepak was not that kind of investor. Deepak was in the business of making many small investments in companies at a very early stage, all at one time. I imagine he knew many of them would fail, so to spend too much time with any one of them could be a waste.

Once, I visited his office in Bangalore during our negotiations, in one of the most strained times of our negotiation process, with my iPhone set to 'record' and laid face down on his desk, which I knew was illegal. I wanted to make sure I had proof he had committed to the term we were discussing just in case he wanted to renegotiate it at some later date. I looked up at a large whiteboard hanging in his office and noticed he had over thirty names of startups written in blue dry-erase marker.

'Is that your pipeline?' I asked.

Deepak shook his head yes, 'You won't believe how many deals I look at every day.'

While we spoke over ten minutes, he got at least three phone calls that he had to take, and two people walk in to ask him urgent questions. Perhaps he was so busy that he mixed up the terms he agreed to with different startups.

I'm not sure, I can only guess, but for me, the negotiations were the most awful months of my life. I had never been treated with such blatant disregard; it felt as if he thought he was doing me an immense favour by investing in my company.

I am sure I was awful for him too. I was brought up in America, after all, so perhaps I was not the demure and deferential young woman that he expected.

I thought a lot about my mom, in those days.

◈

When I was nine-years-old, Mom decided it was time I started learning how to be a good wife, mother and daughter-in-law. The tradition in our family for generations was patriarchal: women were expected to care for the home, the food, the elders and the children, while men were expected to pay for all of it. So, when I was nine, like a young geisha in training, I started to learn some of the tricks of my mother's trade.

Mom taught me to make roti and subzi, she taught me to sing, dance, and play Indian classical music, she taught me to stitch clothes and sew buttons onto shirts, she taught me to tie a sari, she taught me to iron and she taught me to make the perfect chai. Mom taught me all of this while Yogi, five years older than I, played video games and went to tennis practice. It wasn't that he didn't have chores too – he took out the garbage and cleaned the dishes after dinner – but it seemed like there was some invisible line between what I was being taught to do and what he was.

It didn't strike me as particularly unfair at the time because that's just how it worked in our house, and it seemed like mastering those skills would give me access to a club, *The Good Wives' Club*, that I felt desperate, even at nine, to get access to one day. 'You're so thin and tall, beta! One day you'll marry a nice rich man and we'll have a big wedding for you. Nazar na lage,' an aunty would say to me at a party, shoving her ring finger into the crease of her eye to grab a small dab of black eyeliner and press it into the side of my neck. *May this black dot protect you from the evil eye*.

What was unique about our household though, as compared to many Indian families around us, was that Mom was not like the other aunties in *The Good Wives' Club*.

Although Mom taught me all these skills because they would lead me to the safe option – the comfortable home in the suburbs with the gainfully employed husband, two obedient kids attending private schools nearby, and a mother-in-law in the guest bedroom happily sipping on her ginger-chai – Mom had quietly taken a different path herself.

My mother and my father met each other through an arranged marriage in Punjab coordinated by their parents. As a child, I often imagined their first meeting, both silent participants in what I imagined was an awkward living room discussion between their parents over chai and mithai. As the story goes; Mom was lined up next to her two unmarried sisters in her green salwar-kameez, looming taller and lankier than the rest. She was nineteen-years-old, five-foot-eight and weighed less than one hundred pounds, but she had beautiful, playful eyes that would change from blue to green depending on the shade of her outfit that day.

Shortly after her wedding, Mom moved from her small town in Punjab to a house in a suburb of San Francisco with my father, his many siblings and his parents. Although she portrayed the qualities of a young woman who was demure and deferential – a woman who had accepted her fate as a housewife, a mother, and a caretaker to her in-laws – my mom had other plans on her mind as well.

After enrolling in a local college and completing her degree in engineering, Mom found a job at Adobe. While rearing two young children, cooking a three-course-meal every night, and caring for her husband's family, my mom then decided to start her own company.

Mom built her business out of our garage at first, just on Sundays with a small handful of clients, just like Steve Jobs and Wozniak did. She knew back then that many immigrant parents were worried that their children might lose their connection to their motherland. So, she started a class that taught the Hindi language and Indian culture to the children and the children's children of Indian immigrants, of which our suburb had plenty.

Today, at sixty-two-years-old, Mom still successfully runs that business and it's her primary income generator. She now has a handful of trained teachers teaching Hindi to hundreds of students across the Bay Area. In early 2018, an investor offered millions to buy her business from her. Mom declined.

When I was ten-years-old, I remember waking up one Sunday morning dreaming of the Sunday that the Brady Bunch kids used to get on TV. Stacks of pancakes drizzled with maple syrup, fresh squeezed orange juice, Tom and Jerry cartoons on the TV, and Mom wearing a white apron in the kitchen humming a happy tune with a big smile on her face. As I pulled back the covers from my bed and slowly laboured down the stairs towards the kitchen, I could smell the syrup and butter steaming off the pancakes, and I could hear the cartoons emanating from the television.

When I got downstairs, the kitchen was empty, and Mom was in the garage teaching ten sleepy ten-year-old kids their ka-kha-ga-ghas.

I felt abandoned. I felt lied to.

This was not the kind of mother Mom taught me to be outwardly. I thought moms were supposed to wait on their husbands and children. I thought moms were supposed to have no priority that trumped that of her family's needs. I felt jealous, though, too. Mom seemed genuinely happy when she stepped out of our house and into the garage; her office and classroom. Mom stayed up for hours into the night correcting her students' homework, with a smile on her face the entire time.

Tradition dictated that Mom behave a certain way – as a housewife and caretaker first – but Mom built a startup from scratch with no funding and no support whatsoever. Many nights, Mom would be grading Hindi homework and Dad would walk into the room and yell, 'Hindi again? Can't you do anything besides Hindi?' Dad was jealous too. But Mom didn't care. Hindi was her passion, and she came alive when she was running her business.

Mom would never have called herself a feminist or entrepreneur when I was growing up, but in her own patient and dogged way, perhaps without even realizing or intending it, she taught me her own unique definition of the words.

◈

I had met plenty of feminist Indian women throughout my five years of living in India, but we all seemed to hold a silent agreement that we'd hide our feminist stripes when push came to shove, especially when it came to fundraising. Most of us, including myself, over hundreds of investor meetings, had never met a female investor. Female investors were a rare breed, and only one woman I knew of, Vani Kola, was actually *running* a fund in India at the time: Kalaari Capital. A man who worked at that fund in the education portfolio had already rejected me, and I never got to meet Vani.

Every single pitch I gave was to a room full of men – some younger than me, some twice my father's age – and none of them could truly understand what it felt like to be a young mom in India. They would nod along, saying they understood what their wives or sisters had to deal with while scanning me with their beady eyes, but these men were at work until at least 6 or 7 p.m. every night, so their child's afterschool activities, which typically happened from 3 to 6 p.m., was not a huge concern for them.

Surprisingly, of the nine other small investors I had wrangled small amounts of capital from, two were women, but this would be one of their first forays into startup investing. That meant that they would probably not add that much non-financial value to the business, although I didn't know that at the time. Being a great early-stage investor takes a lot of work, it turns out.

When I felt the worst I've ever felt about myself during the negotiations with Deepak, I would swallow my pride and tell myself, he's all I've got, and he's all I'll get.

There were certain terms Jonathan would just not let me give in to, though.

'He cannot have right of first refusal,' Jonathan said. 'Give him right of first offer.'

'What's the difference?'

'ROFR means he has the right to match anyone's new investment offer in the future. So, if Sequoia makes you an offer in your next round, Aarin can make the same offer and you'd have to take it from them. ROFO means he simply gets the first chance to make an offer in a new round, but after that it's your call who you go with.'

'Why does it matter so much what happens in future rounds? I just need money today, right now.'

'It will matter in the future, you're going to need money again, right?'

'I can't even think that far out. I can only think about tomorrow and how I'm going to pay my team their salaries.'

'Well, I'm not letting you agree to a ROFR. That's not fair to your business.'

'Alright, let me call Deepak.'

◈

This was how most of my conversations went with Jonathan in those days, leading me into battle with Deepak with my head held high, only to walk off the battle field bloodied and feeling guilty.

'You have no appreciation for what we're doing for you,' Deepak would say. 'Why are you nit-picking on every minor detail?'

'Deepak, we are just negotiating terms, these details are important to me.'

'You need to focus on growing your business, not on arguing with me all the time. You won't find a better offer out there. Take my offer or leave it, I don't care anymore. I can't wait much longer. Sign it and grow your business, or don't and let it die.'

◈

I started to believe him, too. I believed I wouldn't find anyone else with better terms, and I was confident all those people who originally said no, but then said yes, would back out without Mohandas Pai's name on the dotted line.

So, I agreed to Deepak's terms, and signed the legal investment agreement on 31 March and waited for the money to come in.

◈

Then, out of nowhere, GJ quit. It completely blindsided me. We had just closed our first round of investment capital, I was paying salaries again, and the future was looking good for once. It didn't make sense, why now? How could he do this to us? To me?

I did not handle it well at all. It's one of the bigger regrets and failures I have made as a CEO and mentor at KleverKid. I saw GJ leaving us at such a pivotal moment in the business as pure betrayal. He was my go-to-guy, my mother squirrel, he handled the entire merchant listing process, what would I do without him?

What I should have been asking myself is: why wasn't he happy here? What can I learn from his departure?

Having a respected, loyal employee and good friend leave my company should have been an opportunity for me to grow as a leader and mentor, but instead, I shunned him. I was riding an all-time ego high, so with very few formalities or words between us, GJ left KleverKid.

◈

A few weeks later, I was flown out to Silicon Valley to speak to the students and parents at my old high school, Harker, about entrepreneurship and social impact. Harker was like the children's Harvard of the Bay Area – elitist, exclusive and entitled – but none of that mattered to me by this point. What mattered was that I was being honoured by a school, by the very same people, that suspended and nearly kicked me out due to bad grades and poor behaviour fifteen years ago. Many friends in my small group had been expelled, and my graduation from there was more a sigh of relief than it was a proud moment for me.

I hated that school. But my parents pulled me out of public school and put me into this, the most expensive private school in Silicon Valley that ranks within the top fifty most expensive schools in the country, because they were worried about me. I was doing fine at the time, but I wasn't the best, and things could take a turn for the worse anytime, they must have thought.

I think my parents worried I'd end up doing drugs, failing my classes, and worst of all, not getting into college if I stayed in public school. Yogi had attended public school five years before me and dallied in some of these vices, but he's a fulltime AirBnB host and part-time Yoga instructor now, making more money than I could ever dream of. He's also married, he has the kind of Zen calm I've only seen in Buddhist monks, and he has a curious and courageous little daughter named Sereena. So, I think it's safe to say that the public-school system did not fail him. Fremont is a wealthy city and the public schools rank in the top ten in the state of California and in the top 100 in the country. We were not living in a slum.

But I begrudgingly attended Harker for four years and I tried to like it when I was a teenager in the early 2000s. I made new friends, learned how to search AskJeeves (the first Google), write HTML code, and use Photoshop – skills I still use to this day – and found a soccer coach who became an inspiration, mentor and friend.

When I got up on stage on 10 April in front of packed audience of students, teachers, and parents currently affiliated with Harker, I talked about failure. Harker does not teach you to fail, I said. Harker teaches you to succeed. But here's the hitch, I said.

'If you never learn to fail, you will never succeed.'

Chapter Six

'A startup puts you on an emotional rollercoaster unlike anything you have ever experienced. You flip rapidly from day to day one where you are euphorically convinced you are going to own the world, to (one) in which doom seems only weeks away and you feel completely ruined.'
— Marc Andreessen

By the time I returned from Silicon Valley, I had mailed the physical investment document around to all the investors, who lived across India and the United States, and we were in the process of collecting signatures. In May 2015, it was all signed, sealed and delivered. Luckily, with the money Deepak had loaned me, I was able to back pay my team for the missed January salaries as well as cover February, March and April salaries from the loan. I would just pay the loan money back to Aarin once the investment capital came in May.

When the actual investment capital from all the investors hit the bank, Rupees 1.4 crore, almost a quarter of a million dollars, I felt both proud and paralyzed at the same time. Based on Uma's advice, we put out a press release announcing the investment. Hundreds of friends, family members and journalists reached out to me with congratulations and asking for comment. *This must mean I'm a success, right? Everyone thinks I'm a success now, so I must be a success.*

Our business was growing at a solid pace by May; on 8 May, we saw over 1,000 users visit our website – the most we had ever seen on our website in one day – and we celebrated with Kingfisher beer on the balcony. Things were going well for us now.

By this point, PK had moved us into a new office space. After signing the lease with a cantankerous ninety-year-old grandma ready to kick the bucket, we realized the office was infested with termites and had to be completely torn down inside, fumigated, rebuilt and repainted while we sat on a solitary desk in the centre of the room pinching our noses against the fumes.

PK and I had started interviewing dozens of candidates for key roles we wanted to fill right when the funding hit the bank. We knew we needed a head of merchant sales to focus on growing the seller side of the marketplace and a head of offline marketing to expand the buyer side of the marketplace in malls and events, since Saif was focused on online marketing on Facebook and Google. We also knew we needed someone to focus on city growth – by that time, GJ had listed hundreds of merchants from all over Delhi but with him gone, our listing growth was stagnating – but the funding we had raised was supposed to be used primarily on growth to a new city: Bengaluru.

In hindsight, growth to a new city at this stage was a poor decision for many reasons. First, we had not proven ourselves in the Delhi market yet, and Delhi NCR was massive. There was Delhi, Gurgaon and Noida which held a total of 46,000,000 people. Over the month of May, we saw 9,000 unique visitors on our site. We still had a long, long way to go in NCR. Worse, we hadn't figured out how to make money in NCR.

We were operating on fear and impatience though. According to my financial model, this seed capital of a quarter of a million dollars would last us twelve months, but I had just reduced that timeline by four months due to the back pay I had to fulfil from January until April. So, starting May, we actually only had eight months of a runway before we would be broke again, and I knew that at least six months before that broke-date, I would need to show *much better* growth metrics to start convincing a new, larger investor to invest in a Series A round with us. The next time I raised capital I did not want to wait until the last moment to start talking to investors. That meant practically speaking, I had two months to grow rapidly.

In hindsight, raising only enough capital to buy me two months of growth time and eight months of total runway was another extremely poor decision I made. I was desperate to close the round and get the money in the bank, and if I'm honest, I think I would have been willing to close the round with even less capital. But I should have waited and raised more money in that first round.

It was going to be nearly impossible to show sustainable growth within two months in a business like this – marketplaces are built slowly through great user experience which builds customer loyalty and word-of-mouth referrals. And since *sustainable* growth was clearly not an option, I was left with the only other option: unsustainable growth. That meant paid advertising, paid user growth, and basically acquiring hundreds of thousands of new users by hook or by crook.

◈

PK and I had assumed, based on our investors' advice and our own anecdotal experiences, that Bengaluru had a more vibrant, young-couple, migrant population who would be more reliant on a website like this if it existed there, and who was more tech-savvy than the NCR couples. They'd have credit cards and they'd rely on the internet to find classes for their kids.

This was a strikingly different picture from Delhi, where we saw families living in societies that held their own afterschool programmes. Sending kids to programmes within the society was much more convenient for parents rather than driving them somewhere outside the compound. Also, Delhi families seemed to rely heavily on grandparents for afterschool care, which, apparently, Bengalurueans did not do. Mohan, Uma, Deepak, Pranav, Sid, and even Ananda, the second largest investor in our seed round, were all from Bengaluru. They clearly knew more than I did.

So, we started building our expansion plan. Bengaluru first, then we'd head to Mumbai, another large metro with migrant couples and new parents who needed high-quality childcare and afterschool classes. Rapid hiring and rapid growth were two similarly difficult challenges, but to take them on simultaneously was a fool's errand.

Gotta stay hungry, and stay foolish, I thought.

◈

PK and I had a brilliant idea for hitting our rapid hiring and rapid growth targets over the summer in GJ's stead without spending too much cash: we would hire interns. Colleges in India were becoming more open to startups recruiting for internships as compared to the standard IT consulting internships. I was friends with a professor from IIIT-D, a new engineering college that was finding its footing in Delhi at the time.

Interns were cheap, energetic, creative and fun. We had hired one or two in the past to get basic unskilled work done, and now it seemed like a great opportunity to hire low-risk, short-term young people to get a tonne more basic work done. We could hire lots of them, we told ourselves, they would call, take photos and list merchants, and the business would thrive. So, we, a team of three full-time employees at KleverKid, hired eight interns in May.

At the same time, we were narrowing down our pool of candidates for heads of merchant sales and offline marketing. We shortlisted and sent out offers to two people who had graduated from a university in Pune in the same year; Umesh from Delhi for head of merchant sales and Shivani from Bengaluru for head of offline marketing. Magically, they both accepted their offers without too many negotiations and planned to start the same day as the interns, on Monday, 11 May.

In hindsight, starting ten new people on the same day was a bad decision on both PK and my part. While interns are cheap and energetic, they are also young and difficult. They have nineteen-year-old outlooks on life and require a lot of training and handholding to get them up to speed quickly enough to glean value out of them within their three-month internship. Most days during that summer, one or two interns would call in sick, one or two would complain of family issues and another one or two would watch *Game of Thrones* all day at work, eating up our already limited internet bandwidth.

I did the same thing when I was an intern in college, so I should have seen it coming, but I didn't. It was infuriating, so instead of handling it myself, I made PK manage them. PK split up the interns under Shivani, Umesh, Saif and herself. I took one, the engineer, to work on our first Android app.

It turned out that Shivani and Umesh knew each other in college very well. In fact, it turned out they were best friends in college, and when they both started looking around for new jobs earlier in 2015, KleverKid landed in their laps at the exact same time. It was perfect for them – serendipitous even – they had wanted to be in the same city again and working at the same startup would give them ample time to hang out. Years later, to our surprise and joy, they would marry one another.

When PK and I found out they knew each other but never mentioned it to us during the hiring process, at first we had mixed emotions. We felt like maybe we had been used or played. But then we thought, well, what's the worst that could happen? They know each other and they'll get along; sales and marketing *should* get along well. We decided to see it as fortuitous, and for the most part, it was.

By the end of May, we had hired two more full-time employees – Mehul and Karthik for customer support and growth respectively – and we had decked out our office with stylish furniture and good vibes. I had become obsessed with building the 'right' culture at KleverKid.

Our office was the size of a small studio bedroom. We had custom-made wooden desks installed that ran along the walls with post-its describing our half-baked ideas littered on the windows and tables. There were two tall standing-tables in the centre of the main room, with hard round wooden stools that matched. I liked to stand while I worked to keep my body active. Our office had two air conditioners installed, but unless you sat directly beneath them, they didn't exist. Delhi's heat always won, but I didn't mind it, so I assumed everyone else wouldn't mind either.

We put a brand-new, sky-blue couch on one end of the room for meetings, with a small coffee table showcasing Eric Reis's *The Lean Startup* and two white chairs that looked like they came from the set of *Mad Men*. When Saif accidentally sat on an open black pen on the new couch, I yelled at him in front of the entire team for being irresponsible and careless. I even made him hire a cleaner to deep clean the couch over the weekend. So much for good vibes.

For the most part, we were all still a bunch of kids trying to build something cool. When a new-hire joined, we conducted a formal 'welcome party' where we sat the new-hire alone on a stool in the middle of the room, while the veterans sat in a circle around him or her. We'd pepper the new-hire with painfully embarrassing and personal questions about their past. When we were feeling particularly mean, we'd make them answer everything in academic 'shudh' Hindi (a lost art that many Indians, including myself, no longer speak). Then we'd ask them how smart they thought they were. Usually, they'd nervously reply, 'I think I'm pretty smart?'

'Do you think you can name random objects at lightning speed?' we'd ask.

'Any object?'

'Yes, any object.'

'Sure, of course I can.'

Thus began the Tape Game, a game Saif invented in which two people faced off, one new-hire and one veteran, and took turns rapidly naming unique and random objects. The only rule was that you could not repeat any object, and you could not pause in between turns; it was rapid fire. So, the game went like this:

'Lamp!'

'Chair!'

'Window!'

'Laptop!'

'Desk!'

'Lamp!'

Repeat! You lose!

It sounds easy, but when you're awkwardly staring someone in the eyes and have a group of twelve people watching and waiting for you to slip up, it's surprisingly hard. The unexpected difficulty is the beautiful lure of the game. And veterans usually won. The first person to pause or repeat an object was taped. Getting taped took on various forms. One time a new-hire was left mummified from head to torso wrapped in tape. Another time, strong sticky duct tape was applied to a new-hire's eyebrows and upper lip.

We loved to play games and throw parties and drink Kingfisher beer and show up late for meetings (for which I'd force the late person and their entire team to drop and do one push-up per minute late), but we also loved to work hard and put in the long hours to get the important work done. Most days, you could hear bubbling bhangra or swooning Bieber combined with roaring laughter emanating from our windows, pouring into the winding streets of Shahpur Jat, enveloping innocent bystanders with the optimism and excitement of a startup with audacious dreams. Those were the good days, though. At that time, the bad days were few and far between, and they were easier to write off as a fluke.

By the beginning of June, we had launched our new website, had a team of fifteen including the interns, and we were becoming much more familiar with the mechanics of how our business worked and did not work. But we were still failing a lot.

My mantra in the office was always, 'We celebrate failure here.' I even put it in writing in the cover letter on people's employment agreements. It wasn't always as simple as that for me though. I often reminisced during that summer back to when my fear first battled with my alter ego about what failure, and thus success, meant to me.

◇

For the first time in my life, at the age of nineteen, I had failed big. Sure, it was a relatively small failure in the larger scheme of things – I had simply tried to sell a discount card to college students, but could not due to legal issues – but I was nineteen and self-absorbed and I had followed the rules and stayed on the straight and narrow path until then. Surprisingly, my failure had a massive butterfly effect on the people around me that I could not have predicted, which then led to multiplying my own self-doubt and shame.

My father told me to take the failure off my resume and never talk about it in interviews. My mother was worried about my dwindling GPA. My friends stopped going out with me out of fear of another blubbering drunk tirade about how spineless our university was. Holed up in my dorm room on the far side of campus like a lost sock tumbling around in the back of the drying machine, staring at the last remaining mustard-and-black coloured Bargain Steeler Card on my desk, I wondered why this hurt so much.

I started to interrogate my alter ego with questions. *How could I have failed? What does it mean that I failed? How do other people deal with their failures? Has anyone I know ever failed as badly as I just did? Why doesn't anyone ever talk about their failures? What will everyone think when they find out I've failed?* I spent weeks trying to figure out what went wrong, and how I could have avoided failing.

When I came close to graduating college, I started searching for a job in the 'real world'. In one job interview, a tired man with a shiny head sat behind a long mahogany desk and stared down at my resume as I entered the room. He motioned for me to sit across from him.

'So, you're an engineer?' he said.

'Yes…well, no, not yet…but, yes, I'm going to be,' I stammered.

'How many airplanes do you think are flying in the sky right now?' he said.

'Um…well…let's see…hmm…maybe a million?'

'Can you tell me how you got that answer?'

'I honestly just guessed…am I in the right interview? My name is Shabnam Aggarwal. Two Gs.'

'Yes, we like to see how you think.'

'Oh, okay. But what does this role entail?'

'You would be building chips for microprocessors that go inside our phones.'

'I see. So…no planes?'

'No, no planes.'

I quickly realized I had very little interest in building nano-sized computer chips for expensive computing devices, as my undergraduate program and my father would have hoped. I was more interested in figuring out how I could use my technology skills to help kids learn to take big risks and build resilience to overcome difficult situations like the failure I had gone through. It seemed inevitable that every kid would face failure at some point in his or her life, and the most courageous innovators in the world seemed to have the support and tools to pick back up from their failures so they could go on to solve some of the world's most pressing problems: poverty, energy, education, health, and hunger.

Why hadn't anyone taught me how to deal with failure all my life? Why was success the only path I was ever led down? Why was the path of success so narrow and restrictive?

I soon became obsessed with researching failure to try and understand it more deeply. I wanted to diagnose the experience of failure like a doctor conducting a post-mortem. I wanted to get at the emotion of failure; where it comes from, why it's got such a bad reputation, and how we've all learnt to avoid it like the plague.

I thought if I could understand it better, I might be able to craft a model for overcoming it. So, I created a thesis, a theory of change: I believed that if we could teach ourselves to embrace the phases of failure, we could end up achieving much greater success – however we defined it – than if we had avoided failure our whole lives.

Initially, I started out by trying to disprove my theory. It seemed like it flew in the face of everything I was taught, especially in an Indian household like mine. In my house, it felt like our motto was the same as Instagram's: only tell people about the good things going on in your life, the things that will make everyone else jealous of you. Conceal your imperfections and your problems and take them to the grave, or in our case, the crematorium, with you.

So, I took the job on Wall Street like Dad told me to.

◈

After a few years of trying to disprove my theory by following the family motto, in 2010, just after I failed with MILLEE and felt the familiar sensation of shame and embarrassment, I found myself back on the quest to understand my fear of failure.

I had taken a risk leaving Wall Street for Cambodia and again leaving Cambodia for India – a few small steps towards finding my purpose and passion – but I was financially safe the whole time. I moved only after I had secured a job that paid me enough to survive comfortably in those places. *Why was I still so unwilling to take a big risk with my life? What was I so afraid of?*

It seemed like the one group of people who were yet unaffected by the shame and fear of failure were babies. I enrolled in an online course with a famous child psychologist named Alison Gopnik teaching at UC Berkeley.

I pored over her lectures, books and talks. Gopnik has a powerful and musical voice and she can tell stories that will make you laugh and cry and wonder within minutes. She can even hold your attention while talking about some pretty dry human psychology stuff. The one thing that struck me from her lectures was when Gopnik talked about how babies approach everything around them with awe. Babies are like 'tiny brilliant scientists,' Gopnik said. She found a fascinating correlation between a species' intelligence, and the amount of time that species spends as a 'dependent child' learning about the world before they're able to be self-sufficient. No species takes longer to become self-sufficient than humans do.

One day, around that time in 2010, I was visiting my family in Fremont and playing with my three-year-old niece, Sereena, in the front yard of my childhood home. My brother was on his cell phone nearby while he watched me try to teach Sereena to ride a tricycle.

I sat her down in the seat and held on tight to the back of the cycle. I wrapped each of her small hands around the handlebars and told her to try and move the pedals forward with her feet while I held on.

Sereena was small, but she got the hang of it quickly. She started pedalling faster and faster and when I felt like she could move without my holding on, I let go.

The second she noticed I had let go, she turned her head back to look for me, got scared, and the entire cycle started to tip in one direction. I ran behind her to try to save her from the fall but I was one second too late, and she crashed onto the ground. Yogi sprinted over, peeled his daughter off the ground, and while whispering a few angry words at me, squeezed Sereena tight as she started to wail.

Although I didn't offer my brother my scientific assessment at the time, it occurred to me that, like Gopnik said, my niece had an idea in her head about the way the world worked – that she could turn back to look for me while staying balanced on her cycle – and then she went after trying to prove her theory, but to no avail.

When she fell off the cycle, she, as a tiny scientist in that moment, had not 'failed,' but had learned something new. She had added knowledge to her theory about the world. She had developed her brain, her heart, and she had toughened her metaphoric skin. In learning what did and did not prove her latest theory, she was embarking on her effort to successfully grow up and learn about the world.

At the same time, just as she learned something new, she also felt the power of fear. She immediately saw her actions, her research, her experiments-gone-wrong, lead to the consequence of causing pain to herself and to others around her: others she deeply admired and loved, others who cared for her and loved her, others who she depended upon for her safety and security.

In this way, she learned the consequences for having failed. She caused this painful, negative emotion and she began to fear causing it again.

By contrast, when she had leaned off her rear end at thirteen-months, wobbled into surfer stance, and finally took her first steps after weeks of trying, she observed the power of pride and happiness. She watched her actions, research, and experiments-gone-well, lead to the outcome of happiness and excitement for herself and everyone around her.

My niece was beginning to hone her understandings about the world, and move in and out of what the psychologist Lev Vygotsky calls the 'Zone of Proximal Development', or what I call, more simply, the 'Zone of What I Cannot Yet Do', into what I call the 'Zone of What I Can Do Now' which is an amazing feeling as a baby, and as an adult.

My niece learnt, almost from the moment she was born, what her effect could be on herself, and perhaps more importantly, on those around her, when she 'failed' as compared to when she 'succeeded'.

◈

I became so immersed in the study of babies that later that year I applied to a small preschool teacher-training programme in Pune so that I could spend more time observing and learning about how babies think and grow. It turned out I was not a natural toddler whisperer, but the programme changed my world view completely. Until that point I had believed that technology alone could solve all the problems we had in education and inequality – but while crafting fifteen-minute lesson plans for a class of three- and four-year-olds, I realized technology alone would never teach us how to fail, how to pick back up, how to learn from our failure, and how to try again. We learn that from the people around us –

our parents, teachers and coaches – and no amount of technology could ever replace that pivotal and ongoing lifelong lesson.

I slowly began to feel like I understood how babies learned to approach and deal with failure, and what it might take to help more people embrace failure. So, I started sketching a graph of what the experience of failure truly looked like before, during and after.

What I still didn't have a good understanding of was whether this fear of failure was unique to just me, just my culture, or even just my generation. I knew I had been born to Indian immigrants who had a lot to lose when coming to America, but I felt like everyone I knew was trying, in some way or another, to weave their story of success while suppressing their stories of failure.

One weekend in 2011, I visited Boulder, Colorado, one of the wealthiest and most 'successful' cities in the US. I asked my friend, Larissa, to grab some video equipment and join me to interview random people on the streets about their experiences with failure.

'Can you tell me about the last time you seriously failed at something?' I asked a young, well-built white man in his late twenties, standing next to his girlfriend, squeezing her hand tight.

'Well, yes, but I've never talked about it before,' he said.

'What happened?' I asked.

'This makes me a little uncomfortable, but what the heck. I was in the air force a few years ago, and my crew and I were loading bombs onto the back of a fighter plane. I was responsible for setting up the loading equipment, but I guess my brain wasn't working very well that day, or maybe I was just tired from not having much sleep. One minute we were loading the bombs and the next thing I knew, the loading equipment slipped out and a bomb dropped almost a whole story to the ground. I watched it fall like it was in slow motion; confident my life was about to end. By some crazy luck, the bomb didn't detonate, but I never recovered from that experience. I couldn't sleep for months and I became anxious every time I had to do anything involving the bombs. I worried about the people whose lives I could have ended, and their families back home,' he said. His shoulders slumped over and he wiped his free palm over and over, leaving a swelling circle of a sweat on his khaki pant leg.

'Whoa. That's a pretty scary event. How did you overcome it?' I said.

'Honestly, I don't know if I ever really did. We didn't have a culture of talking about our anxieties or failures in the air force so I had to pretend like it never happened.'

'What did you do after that?'

'I left the air force soon after that, and now I work as an independent graphic artist.'

'Do you have any regrets about the experience?'

'Obviously, I wish I hadn't been so tired while I was loading bombs! But, more than that, I wish I had a way to get past it, somehow. I wish I could have talked to someone who could have told me it wasn't my entire fault, or that I was still good at what I did. I felt really ashamed.'

'Was there anything that stayed with you from the experience? Did it add any value to your life?'

'Yea, I made some suggestions to my commander about how to prevent the same thing from happening again, and I heard they've actually implemented my suggestions. It also made me realize I didn't want to work in a place that was so unsupportive. I needed more freedom and I wasn't passionate about bombs or the air force. It caused me to find this new path that is much more fulfilling to me. But most of all, it showed me that I could do some pretty scary stuff, and even if things went totally wrong, I'd be able to overcome it.'

◈

I came home that night after interviewing dozens of people on the street all day, and put a question up on my Facebook page: 'Does anyone else feel like they failed and have nowhere to share it?'

Hundreds of people responded.

One man, Billy Valentine, wrote to me, 'Some of my failures are so deep and personal that they have shaped my life profoundly. Some failures have been devastating to the point of depression and persistent thoughts of suicide. Some have been largely due to my [own] contribution, and some have been more circumstantial or situational.

'It is this set of failures that has shaped me into the tenacious and unrelenting pursuer of my interests. This has driven me to work harder and with more passion than ever before. And that level of dedication, when applied to a situation that is more conducive to success, has yielded excellent results.'

One woman, Joanna Hawley, wrote, 'After about two years I became very burnt out and started feeling extremely depressed. I struggled to push back on the expectations and make time for self-care, including seeing a therapist, but my boss wouldn't even approve me needing time off. After about six months like that, she fired me. It was a total blow and I had no idea it was coming. That was about four years ago and I still think of it [often]. Now that I'm self-employed and run my own business, I've really taken that experience to heart. The biggest takeaway I've had from it is to communicate constantly and consistently with the people who work for me. I don't want them to ever feel like they are in the dark or totally alone. Instead, I want my company to feel like a place where they can bring their own ideas, take care of themselves and enjoy the work that they do for me.'

Many others sent me long personal essays about their failures, how awful it felt to have to hide it from everyone, how the hiding and shame led them to depression, and how difficult it was for them to climb out without anyone to talk to about it, especially because they had to pretend they were still successful. I realized that just like mine, the experience of failure had been traumatic for a lot of people, causing them to become extremely emotional and leave them reminiscing about a painful memory they had locked away in a hidden drawer of their mind. Many of these people had never talked to anyone about their failure, let alone forgiven themselves for it. They were often stunned by the words that came out of their own mouth, and surprised that the experience and the resulting shame was still affecting them so deeply.

Often, the people I spoke to who had experienced what they considered a major failure in their life had actually changed their life path significantly after their failure. It wasn't always career related. Some had failed in marriage, school, friendships, car accident, or by being arrested; everyone had their own definition for 'major failure'. They did not always attribute their life change to the failure directly, but they were thankful for the course correction that the failure eventually afforded them.

As I interviewed more and more people over 2011, I noticed there was a sequence of events that emerged that were common and matched my own experience of failure. I pulled out my graph sketch and tweaked the model every few days, as I heard more stories and read more books on this topic. Eventually, this is the model I ended up with.

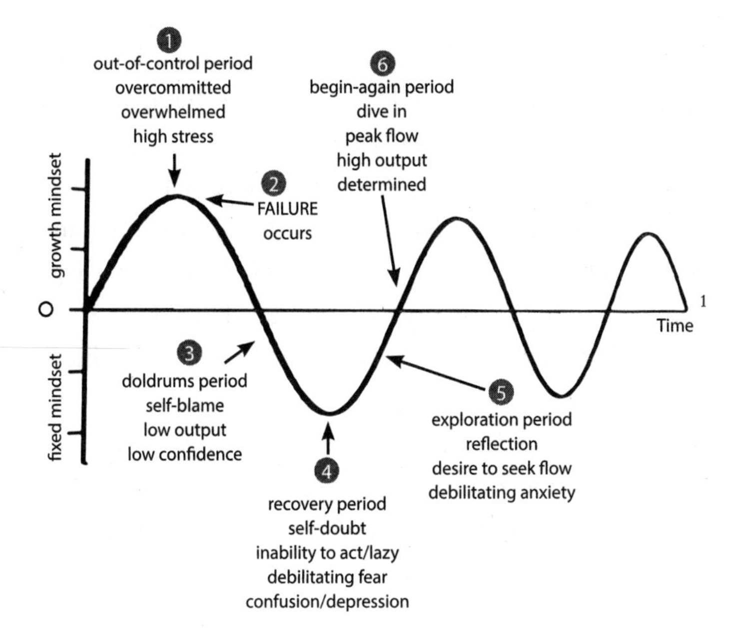

At the time, in 2011, after I finished the preschool training course and built my model for embracing failure, I realized my personal definition of success was

---

1 This model is built around ideas introduced by Alison Gopnik, Adam Grant, Angela Duckworth, Carol Dweck, and Mihaly Csikszentmihalyi. Growth Mindset is a concept that Dweck believes can be learned and embodied by any of us, which I agree with. In my experience, though, we oscillate from fixed to growth mindset depending upon where we are in the recovery process.

taking shape. I thought, at the time, that success would be if I were directly responsible for changing millions of children's lives.

Directly, because I wanted the recognition; I wanted to be famous, like Mother Teresa. Millions, because it was a number that sounded really big.

After all my research, I knew that to achieve great things, I needed to be fearless, take risks, tackle big and difficult challenges, fail a lot, and eventually, perhaps then, I'd be able to call myself a success one day.

But somehow, in my first endeavour to achieve success, after I failed with the Bargain Steeler Card at CMU, I noticed I had begun to shun my tiny scientist within. I started choosing the slightly easier route, the one with lesser unknowns and lower potential to fail. I chose to work on Wall Street after college instead of volunteering for the Peace Corps in rural Kenya. I challenged myself only as much as necessary, only as much as felt comfortable; I avoided meeting new people, so I hung out with high school and college friends after work for drinks at swanky bars downtown. I let my thirst for an undefined success call the shots, and I let my fear of failure hold me back from taking the big risks.

◈

One day, at the KleverKid office in the middle of June, PK and I were sitting in one corner of the office discussing the next big risk we wanted to take: paid advertising. Since we knew we had to grow rapidly over the next three months, and time was running out, we agreed it was time to find a paid digital marketing expert. Shivani was great with offline marketing at malls, events and conferences, and Saif was great with branding and SEO, but they both had no experience in analytics, digital marketing and paid ads.

We told the team to keep their eyes peeled for friends or friends of friends who were experts in digital marketing. A week later, a boy named Shayon walked into our office for an interview. I say boy because when I first saw him walk through the door, I thought he couldn't be more than eighteen-years-old. Shayon was short with a baby face and a sweet smile. He sat down on the light blue couch and opened his laptop in front of me. It had been a long week and I was not interested in hearing a bland pitch, but he came highly recommended and his initial assessment of our analytics data was spot on, so I took a deep breath and let him start his pitch.

Shayon, from that moment on, never ceased to impress me. That evening he walked me through the most well-researched, well-laid out plan for growing our visitor numbers, cleaning up our search engine optimization, and with a combination of organic and paid traffic, making us the number one parenting site in India.

I offered him a Kingfisher and asked him when he could start.

I had never hired anyone on the spot before, but I had no doubt in my mind about this young man. He had courage and audacity, and I recognized a hunger for purpose in his eyes when he spoke to me.

Shayon started the next day and stayed with us until the bitter end.

◈

While, on the one hand, in hindsight, I believe the people we hired to work for KleverKid were all individually good decisions, on the other, I believe I grew our team way too fast with much too young of an average age. I strongly believed at the time that everyone could be trained and taught, through a handful of fast failures, to learn to do their job well, but having fifteen to twenty people shoved into one studio-sized office space without much guidance or support led to a lot of false starts and a quickly diminishing confidence.

Whenever I interviewed someone over the age of thirty, I convinced myself they wouldn't be a good culture fit, they wouldn't be able to take the fast pace and long hours I demanded, but in reality, I was scared to hire people who knew more than me. It was my fear talking; my fear of losing control of the business and my fear of putting its future in the hands of someone else kept me from hiring experienced, capable people in those early days. Also,

I wanted to stretch my money as long as possible, and experienced people were expensive.

I didn't make it easy for my young team to hit their stride though.

Every two weeks I would send an update to our ten investors and a few advisors and mentors who wanted to be kept in the loop on the progress of KleverKid. I was also meeting new investors every day throughout that summer. I had learned my lesson from the last fundraise and I wanted to keep my relationships strong so that when I asked someone to invest later, they wouldn't feel like it was out of the blue.

The only problem with this method is that every few days I would hear a reaction from an investor like, 'Your revenue seems oddly low.'

Or, 'Rather than user growth, you should be focusing on merchant listings.'

Or, 'Why aren't there more reviews for the merchant listings on your site?'

Or 'What's your customer acquisition cost these days? Have you brought it down since we last spoke?'

Or, 'Have you tried partnering with FirstCry?'

Every time I heard a response like this, I would run over to bug PK or Shivani or Umesh or Saif or Karthik or Shayon or Mehul. I would derail whatever other work they were doing and force them to focus on this new 'pressing' issue. This must have been excruciatingly annoying and frustrating for them. Here I was, asking them to accomplish their work at lightning speed with no training whatsoever, and on top of that I kept throwing curve balls at them from every angle I could find, with no clarity on how to prioritize or identify if they were doing well or completely failing.

On top of that, every week I held a team 'stand-up' where everyone would go around the room and publicly announce their successes and failures from the past week, along with their targets for the following week. My thinking in holding this stand-up every week was that it would give people a chance to offload their challenges and get support from the rest of the company on a way forward. For example, it was common for the product and sales teams to not speak to one another throughout the week, but at that meeting, the product team might realize that the sales team was struggling to explain and sell a major feature of our product to merchants, thus reducing their sales targets significantly, and affecting the business as a whole. This meant that the product team needed to prioritize that feature, or give sales a better feature they could sell.

If I could go back now, I honestly do not know how I would have handled that summer better. I was subconsciously aware that my team needed a leader with a clear vision and mission and a week-to-week plan that didn't oscillate based on what outside people suggested offhandedly to me. I was desperate for advice.

I was in way over my head; I was also just another twenty-something with almost no leadership experience and no marketplace building experience whatsoever. I wanted so badly to succeed, to be directly responsible for changing a million children's lives. This time, for the first time in my life, it seemed like my goal was in arm's reach. Smart people like Mohandas Pai believed in me, even if my father was still calling it my 'fun little project', I was surviving without my parent's financial support and we had thousands of parents using our website every day trying to find great classes and coaches for their kids. One million children's lives changed felt possible.

◈

By the end of July, I had hired the first two full-time employees of my in-house product team. I hired an engineer and a product manager, Prateek and Victor, both from Bengaluru, to join our team in Delhi. Prateek had some experience with PHP – the language our website was built in – and I was eager to move our product ownership from our external consultant over to an in-house team. *Why, though?*

For one, I was through and through a 'product person'. I was a trained engineer, but more than that, I loved spending my time working on the product – having it outsourced felt like too little control for me. I wanted to be able to walk over to my product team and have them show me how the main call-to-action button would feel with a slightly rounder corner, or how the homepage scroll would look with a sticky navigation bar, or how a timed popup on the search page might feel to a new user.

To say I was obsessive about our user experience would be accurate, but I don't regret that obsession one bit, even to this day. I still believe that users deserve a beautiful, well-thought-out, highly curated experience when they enter a website or physical space.

Due to A/B testing and user analytics, we were in the unique position of being able to offer different experiences to different types of users, and give people an experience on our site that matched who they were and what they cared about on our website. For a young twenty-five-year old mom who had two children between three and five years old and lived in north Gurgaon, we could highlight preschools and toddler programmes in north Gurgaon and we knew she would stick around on our site for a while until she found something good. For a forty-year-old father who was interested in films and had previously searched for guitar classes in JP Nagar, we could highlight music and dance classes and we were confident he would find something useful for his kid through us.

Our statistics over that summer proved our assumptions to be true, for the most part. By the end of August, we saw a 200 per cent increase in all the major metrics since the spring; new users, sessions and pageviews were all over 200 per cent higher than before. Shayon had proved his capabilities in digital marketing in a very short time. The only key metric that had gotten worse since the spring was our bounce rate.

The bounce rate told us how many sessions on our site had zero interactions and zero seconds spent on the page the user landed on; so, the user 'bounced' on and off our site in under 1 second. This is a bad thing; this is one of the scariest metrics for CEOs and digital marketers to watch grow. This meant a user either clicked on an ad, which our company paid Google or Facebook for, and that ad took them to our site but then they left immediately and we lost them as a potential long-term customer, or, this meant a user came to our site looking for something specific and immediately decided they wouldn't find it on our site, so they left.

Bounce rates for websites with valuable and engaging content like the *New York Times* usually ranged from 40 to 60 per cent, whereas a typical search portal like ours' usually ranged from 20 to 50 per cent in 2015. Our bounce rate had jumped from 20 per cent in March to 80 per cent in August.

This should have been a clear red flag. PK and I knew, going into the summer, that our plan was to grow unsustainably for a few months to rapidly acquire more users, but with that big of a change in our bounce rate, we should have known that most of these users would never come back to us – if they found our site useless once, for whatever reason, they were highly unlikely to come back to us again. Instead of building loyalty, we were building frustration.

Worse, we had spent thousands of our hard-earned investment capital on acquiring the wrong users just for the sake of convincing a new investor to invest more capital in us as soon as possible.

It was a fool's errand but we couldn't see the forest for the trees back then. What we should have done was grow slowly, but the other challenge that increased our impatience was that once the new school year started, we knew the high season for booking children's classes would diminish if not disappear entirely. Ours was a seasonal business, which meant we had to work harder and faster during the spring and summer seasons when parents were searching for activities for their kids, so we took a gamble and we spent the money while we were in the midst of a high season, rather than wait around for the following year's high season to come.

Worse, by the end of August we had launched in Bengaluru and we were spending $30,000/month (Rs 18 lakh/month) on team salaries, marketing and office rent, while making revenue of $100/month (Rs 6,000/month). With the money we spent paying everyone's salaries, running ads and paying the rent on our tiny studio-sized apartment office, if we continued at this burn rate, I calculated we would be out of cash again by November.

Our bounce rate and our revenue number told us that although we had 25,000 people visit our website in August, 20,000 were a waste. And of the 5,000 that were not a waste, who were spending actual time searching for classes for their kids, less than 5 were willing to book a class through our site so that we could make commission on the booking. We were getting disintermediated.

I knew marketplaces took a long time to build trust and grow revenue, but we were ten months into this business. If we couldn't get our revenue beyond $100/month soon, we would need a lot more venture capital to survive over the next five years.

The tide was already shifting in venture capital. Investors in early-stage startups had invested more capital in the first half of 2015 than they had in all of 2014, but exits were few and far between, and it was becoming more and more clear that infusing capital into a business without strong unit economics was a losing proposition.

We weren't one of those companies, though, I said to myself.

Chapter Seven

'People say doing a startup is like a marathon. It's actually like a road trip at night with no headlights. You think you're going to Toledo but you're actually going to Miami and you might not have enough gas, so you might need to buy gas from someone who might take you out if you aren't driving well.' — Ben Silbermann

I met up with KC one day at the end of September to tell him about our challenges with revenue when he came up with a novel idea.

Why not partner with Uber?

Mehul, our customer service lead at KleverKid, had noticed that many of the conversations she had with our users on the phone or through our chat engine often ended with a mom saying she would be keen to visit and book the programme she read about on KleverKid, but that she didn't have access to a car, and she only had cash. So she couldn't book it straight away online or through Mehul on the phone.

Uber was making a foray into India and was using every discount and partnership method under the sun to steal market share from a local Indian company, Ola Cabs.

A friend had invited me to Uber's launch party on a ritzy hotel rooftop in Delhi many months ago. I remembered the free-flowing wine and whiskey, the speech the Head of India gave about Uber taking over the world, and the many stunted conversations with Ivy League alumni who were now in charge of Uber's expansion in India. At the time, I hadn't thought the connections could be of any value for KleverKid, so I stuffed the business cards into a growing stack on my desk and didn't think about them for a long time, until today.

If we could just get these moms to these programmes, they could book in person with cash, we would be able to identify which bookings were ours', and we'd be able to re-intermediate ourselves from the chain of events, KC said. We'd be able to realize the revenue we deserved to be making – we were giving free marketing and lead generation to merchants – and this would be a fool-proof way to guarantee a bump in our revenue.

I sifted through the Uber business cards on my desk and called the first number I found.

First, the bait.

'The mom and kid market is huge in India,' I said to the man on the line, 'But Uber isn't winning market share with them because moms are cautious people by nature, and the rape allegation against the Uber driver last year only made things much worse for you. Women need a good reason to switch from Ola to you guys. I have that reason for you.'

'Sounds interesting,' the man said, 'Come in, let's chat.'

We scheduled a meeting for Wednesday and I hung up.

Now, for the hook.

I'd have to convince this executive that offering free rides to KleverKid users would result in an increased user base of paying customers for Uber. The only problem was that if moms didn't have credit cards to pay us, how would they find credit cards to pay Uber? Maybe Uber in India would be willing to accept cash, even though that was strictly against their policy in other countries.

A few days later, I saved and closed the pitch deck that I had been tweaking for this meeting, shut my laptop and booked an Uber ride.

Uber was in a new high-rise building in Gurgaon. There was a large roundabout that deposited well-dressed executives to the curb by the minute. On the 30th floor,

Uber had six flat screen TVs encircling the waiting room playing various ads that Uber was trying on the Indian market.

A young man with a frazzled look on his face came out to the waiting room to escort me to the Uber executive's office.

Chai? He asked.

Coffee, please. I said.

I introduced myself to the exec and sat down. We exchanged pleasantries about the weather and their new office space, then we got down to business.

'You have a PR problem with women in Delhi,' I said. 'Uber has become synonymous with rape, and that correlation can only change through word of mouth. The women who can give you the strongest PR facelift in Delhi are moms. But you can't directly target moms in your marketing, it would be too obvious that you were trying to make up for the rape last year. You need an intermediary – someone who is trustworthy among moms at kitty parties but who can also vouch for the quality and safety of Uber rides. That's where we come in. KleverKid can help you get that boost, but first, we would need you to make some product tweaks.'

'Like what?' the executive asked.

'Moms don't generally have credit cards. Under 10 per cent of the total population in India owns a credit card, and often it's the husband. You have to allow users to pay with cash,' I told him.

'We're trying cash payments out in Hyderabad, it should come to Delhi soon. Is that all you need changed?' he asked.

'No. You need to let the user change their driver without penalty. Some drivers look or sound drunk or seedy or have a bad rating but you charge a hefty penalty for cancelling. That works against building trust.'

'We can't change that feature, it's too risky. What else can I look into?'

'We'd need an API to plug into your product so that our users can book a ride directly through our website or app. That way we can also see how many riders came through our referral.'

'I think we can do that for you but we'd need to see your user numbers first. Anything else?'

'We'd need to make the first ride free for every new user we bring you.'

'Hmm, I'll have to think about that. I'll get back to you.'

'Okay, great. That's all for now,' I said.

'So, tell me something, why are you so focused on education? Why don't you list restaurants and hotels and other things? You'd have a much bigger audience and better revenue opportunities.'

'Because,' I said, 'none of that other stuff actually matters, especially not to me. I couldn't care less about how nice the hotel you're staying in is, or how much incrementally better the food is at one restaurant versus the next. What matters is how well we educate our kids, how easy we make it for them to discover their passion and become masters of their art. Do you really think hotel listings will change the game for India in the long run?'

'Maybe not, but it would probably help your bottom line in the short term,' he responded. 'I have two kids, and I can tell you right now that my wife and I neither look for nor book these kinds of classes for them every day. The kids have one or two programmes for the whole year and they go to those exclusively. So, personally speaking, I wouldn't use your product more than once a year.'

I hated him in that moment, but in hindsight, I know he was making a good point. At the time, I knew my business was seasonal, but my assumption was that parents would book a class at least once *every season*. Summer season has camps, August–November has tutoring and sports, January–April has test prep. Even better, there were always one-off events on the weekends for kids – festivals, carnivals, pottery class, rock climbing, jewellery making. The list was endless. So, maybe this guy was the anomaly, not the norm, I told myself.

I told him I'd think about his advice and tucked it away in a drawer in my brain. I shook his hand aggressively to make a show of my power and strength – as a woman, as an equal, as an entrepreneur – and left his office.

◈

As I waited on the curb of the office for my Uber driver to arrive, I called Ravi.

'How much do we have left, Ravi?' I asked.

'My latest numbers show we still have until November, so about two months of cash left, have you talked to Aarin about putting more money in?'

'Yea, they said maybe,' I said. 'I need to hold a board meeting and see what everyone can put in.'

'Maybe you should go down there and chat in person,' Ravi said. 'They might be more swayed.'

'That's a good idea,' I said. I thought about having to walk into Deepak's office again, having to sit across the table from him and ask, beg even, for more money, more time, just a little more time. I felt sick.

I was exhausted; emotionally, physically and intellectually. I felt like every day, I was running towards a new, ticking time bomb that I had to defuse just seconds before everything around me blew up, like Priyanka Chopra in that TV show, *Quantico*. Once I'd defuse one, I'd look up and realize there was another one I needed to get to immediately before it blew up as well. They were littered everywhere around me and there was never enough time to stop and get them all at once. Often PK would get to a bomb before me and handle it. Or, the bomb would explode, and together we'd clean up the mess and decide what to do next.

I thought about how different this felt from training for the marathon I ran in 2008 in Washington D.C. At the time, I thought it was the hardest thing I would ever do in my life. I changed my diet, my friends, my sleep schedule, my vacations and left my deadbeat boyfriend. I trained for nine long months, waking up at 6 a.m. every day to either run a handful of miles around Central Park in the middle of New York City, or pack my bag for the two-hour boxing class I'd take in downtown after work. On weekends, I'd run for hours by myself, listening to nothing but my feet hitting the pavement and the wind slapping the trees.

I stopped drinking alcohol, I cut out sugar and oily foods from my diet and all my vacations went to running shorter training races in different cities, so that I would be mentally, emotionally and physically ready for race day.

At the same time, I was responsible for raising $2,620 in donations, $100 for every mile of the race, that would go to needy children's education in India, with an organization called Asha for Education. When I finally raised the full amount, it was the largest sum of money I had ever pulled together in support of something meaningful. I ran the full marathon in October of 2008, and a few days later I quit my job on Wall Street, moved to Cambodia to 'find myself', and I never looked back at that life.

The one thing that felt so different about this challenge with KleverKid was the lack of control. Training for the marathon was 100 per cent in my control. A tough run on any given day was my own fault – I had overeaten or under-slept – and I could fix that problem on my own. With KleverKid, nothing ever felt like it was in my control. I could never fix a problem entirely on my own, and I never knew how to prepare for the next day. Every single day was different, unpredictable and difficult.

◈

I called Uma from the Uber ride on my way back to our office.

'We're going to need more money, what should I do?' I asked him.

'How are the numbers looking?' Uma asked.

'We've grown 3x since May on every single metric, except the revenue is still low. I think I just struck a deal with Uber though! They're going to partner with us, and maybe even offer free rides to our users. We just need more time to get some product changes out, and things should be smooth sailing from there.'

'Okay, let me talk to Mohan. When's the board meeting again?'

'Friday,' I said. 'Thanks Uma. Call me after?'

'Roger.'

⟐

I sat into the sticky, sweaty backseat of the Uber taxi with the windows rolled down because the AC was broken and it was still September. Delhi in September is hot, but more bearable than the summer months. The time it takes to travel from Delhi to Gurgaon, often over two hours in traffic, used to give me anxiety. I couldn't bear the thought of being away from my computer and my team for that long.

Today, it gives me respite. I think back to the first rickshaw ride I tried to hail in India, when I moved from Cambodia to Hyderabad on 20 October in 2009. I walked out the front door of the small hostel I had rented a room from, into the dark alley littered with garbage, stray dogs and human shit. I hadn't walked down the alley more than 100 feet when a motorcycle screeched around the bend up ahead and headed straight towards me. *Act like a local*, I told myself. I had learned the cardinal rule of expatriates while living in Cambodia. Don't shriek, don't cower, act confident.

The blur of the motorcycle with a dim headlight pointed at my face became clearer. Were there three men on this bike? It looked like there were three grown men sitting on the motorcycle, crotches pressed up against one another, yelping something indecipherable and heading directly towards me. Keep your head down, don't stop, don't worry.

In a flash, just 5 feet before reaching me, the three men stuck their arms straight out as if on cue, and one by one, they each slapped my breasts as if my breasts were two tablas waiting to be played by school kids. They laughed and high-fived as they sped off behind me, leaving me frozen on the side of the dark street in Banjara Hills, trying to make sense of what just happened.

My first thought was, *is it what I'm wearing? Did I ask for this? Is it my fault?*

◈

'Yahaan theek hai, Madam?'

I was jolted back to current day by the Uber driver's question. *Is right here fine?* I looked up at my office, I thanked him and I exited the cab. Uma's name popped up on my phone.

'Okay, I have some good news for you, Shabnam.'

'Oh, that's great, Uma. What's up? What did they say?'

'Mohan said he's invested with a few others in a new fund called Saha Fund that will invest specifically in female entrepreneurs. He thinks they should be open to investing in the next round, but you should meet them and get things rolling. You don't have much time.'

'Do you know who's running the fund?'

'Two women, one is young like you, named Ankita, and the other is Usha.'

'Ah, right, I think I've talked to Ankita before. I'll send her a note.'

'Sounds good. Also, come to Bengaluru as soon as possible, maybe even for the board meeting on Friday. We can all meet and chat and see if we can finalize next steps.'

'Okay, let me try.'

◈

I flew to Bengaluru for the board meeting on Thursday and met Ankita, Usha, Uma, Mohan, Ananda, Pranav and Deepak. Mohan called me into his office first thing.

'What's happening with your revenue numbers, Shabnam?'

'They're low, but we're working on it. Our user numbers are looking strong.'

'You need to work harder, find a better revenue model; I can't keep funding you indefinitely.'

'I know, Mohan Sir.'

'Fine. I won't be in the board meeting today, Deepak will take my place. He will help you figure this mess out. Also, if Saha makes an offer, you should take it. Don't argue with them like you did before with us. You need to focus on your business.'

I thanked Mohan and walked out of his room. I never saw him again after that meeting.

I entered the large conference room in Aarin's office to set up my computer and pull up the financial model I had painstakingly put together and maintained over the past year. This was the same model that every VC asked to see, but none knew how to read. This was the model that I sent around to all my investors every two weeks, but which none read before making business-altering suggestions about how we should proceed.

It was a complex model, after all. I had built it with KC and Jonathan's help, and it had, at one point, twenty different tabs worth of financial information and projections for the next ten years of the business. In every single scenario, even in the worst-case scenario, KleverKid turned profitable by the end of 2016. That meant all we really needed was twelve more months of investment capital. To be safe, I'd ask for eighteen today.

This was an awfully naive perspective to take. Can you imagine if, back in 2005, Zuckerberg were to raise 'just enough for the next twelve to eighteen months' in his second round, rather than the $12.7 million he actually raised? Can you imagine where Facebook might be today? It would be nowhere. It would be nothing. We wouldn't have heard of it, and one-third of the population wouldn't spend half our lives scrolling down our news feeds on it today.

Fundraising does not determine 100 per cent of a business's future, but most businesses that make it to the $1 billion valuation Unicorn Club have raised over $1 million by their second round. Fundraising can often separate the would bes from the will bes, and at this point I should have thought bigger. I should have seen the changing VC tide coming, and I should have raised a lot more than I actually did. But I was scared. What if they said no? Then what?

◈

My board members entered the room and sat down in their swivel chairs, ready for battle. I explained the current state of the business, our rapid growth and revenue opportunities, our imminent need for more funding and our plan going forward.

I looked to the projector screen and opened my financial model. The room was silent.

'What are we supposed to look at?' Deepak said.

'Here, you can see our breakdown of costs, the expected revenue and actual revenue we made each month over the last year.' I motioned to the sheet and highlighted the cells with my cursor on my laptop.

'Why are you spending so much money on marketing?' Deepak said.

'Well, it's a marketplace, so we need to market it.'

'Can you cut that cost in half?'

'Sure, but then our user growth will decline.'

'What about this sales cost?'

'Without merchants being "sold" to get listed and share revenue with us, we'd have nothing to sell to the users. But yes, I can try to cut it back.'

'Why don't you try selling to moms through Facebook? Moms are always sitting on Facebook all day.'

'We are trying Facebook, Google, Instagram, Twitter, blogging, partnerships with all sorts of companies like Uber and UrbanClap, referral discounts and even kitty parties. Some have higher CACs with better-quality leads, but we're trying it all. We honestly even tried partnering with a company that literally pays their users fifty rupees to download and use the apps in their app store. It increased our user numbers overnight, but they ended up being mostly nineteen-year-old boys who were very horny and very rude to our customer service people and looking for something entirely different from afterschool educational programmes at 2 a.m. in the morning.'

'Well that's a bad idea. What a waste of money! How could you make such a mistake?'

'Yea, that was a fail for sure. I'm not sure what happened. We were desperate.'

'How's the Bengaluru launch going?'

'Bengaluru is going well, but it has been difficult, to be honest. We only have one person here trying to get things set up, and it's been hard with limited people and a limited network to the afterschool space here. But I am optimistic still. We just need time.'

This was a vast understatement. Bengaluru had not been going well at all. When I visited the one-person team, Karthik, sitting in the back corner of someone else's office again, but this time in Bengaluru, I felt a deep sense of sadness. It was always exciting to get started in a new city, to be able to start from scratch while having learnt from past mistakes, but the situation at this office was dreary at best. This place was not exactly startup culture.

Karthik had planned to run an offline marketing event to drum up interest in Bengaluru, so Shivani, our head of offline marketing, had a bookmark designed that Karthik could pass out at the event. She got hundreds of bookmarks printed at high quality (and a hefty price) and sent them to Karthik the day before his event.

When I sat down next to Karthik's desk, I asked to see the bookmarks he would be passing out the following day. Through all the madness of trying to fundraise and launch and grow, I was less involved in the weeds of design decisions, so I hadn't seen the bookmarks until now.

I took one bookmark out of the stack and admired the design. The colours Shivani had picked were perfect, the animations to explain what we did were spot on, and the quality of the bookmark itself was very good. I could bend and twist it and it did not tear.

But then I noticed something not quite right. The phone number listed on the bookmark, the primary method for someone to get in touch with our team, looked odd. I read it a couple times before realizing that Shivani had accidentally left out one number from our phone number, making it impossible for anyone to reach us. We could not pass these bookmarks out to parents.

I started to unravel. I pulled Karthik over to my desk and demanded an answer. 'How the fuck could this have happened?' I asked him.

Karthik said he wasn't sure, that he hadn't noticed until now, but Shivani had done the design, so I should speak to her.

I took a photo of the bookmark and sent it to Shivani, who was in Delhi, then called her phone over and over until she picked up. 'Shivani, what the fuck? You've just wasted so much money by being careless. How could you not double check every detail of this bookmark? We'll have nothing to give out at the event now. How do you expect to take charge of marketing when you can't even do one simple thing?'

Shivani couldn't imagine how this could have happened. She was stunned.

Worse, I was parroting the style and tone my investors and board used with me – a patronizing, demeaning tone – that often left me feeling like I wanted to throw up. Even worse, I was going back on my word.

In every single person's offer letter, I clearly and overtly stated that at KleverKid, we embraced failure. But here we were, amid dealing with a failure, which in the larger scheme of things wasn't such a huge failure at all, and I was definitely not embracing anyone or anything. I was lashing out, blaming people, and killing their confidence to try something risky and new.

My response to Shivani that day should have been, 'Okay, we failed. What can we learn from it? How might we do things differently next time? What was within our control and what was not? Was this a productive failure or a useless one?'

◈

'What about your revenue numbers, can you show me just those?' Deepak demanded.

'Sure, here they are,' I said, changing the tab over for Deepak in the boardroom. 'As you can see, our revenue is very low – we're seeing many leads visit us, check out a class, even start to book, but then drop off. My hypothesis from chats with users is that they don't want to book until they've seen the place, sized up the teachers, and ensured the security and cleanliness meets their standards. That makes sense, but then once they visit, they book in-person rather than coming back to our app. We get disintermediated. So, we never realize the revenue share from the lead we generated. One way to solve this is to send them a cab so that we're involved in the entire "sizing up" process. Another is to create a merchant dashboard where merchants use our software when booking any new clients.'

'Shabnam, you can't keep messing around anymore, you have to get on track and figure out this revenue issue.'

'I know. I'm trying. I'm sorry.'

I knew it would take time for us to sort out the kinks, but it seemed like we had hit upon something useful – why else were parents visiting us, spending time on our site, and getting all the way to the book button? I couldn't articulate this at the time, but I knew I just needed to find the tipping point for our business. I just needed this to go viral, and our revenue issues would sort themselves out.

I turned to Usha, who sat next to me, looking confused but excited.

'This is a very interesting idea, I think it has a lot of potential, but you'll need to work hard to get it back on track,' Usha said to me.

'Thanks Usha. Is your fund keen to invest in my business?'

'I think we can match whatever Aarin puts into the next round.'

I let out a deep sigh. This was music to my ears. Over the last two months I had already put out feelers with both Deepak and Pranav Pai about whether or not Aarin would be interested in investing in a Bridge Round. They were both positive about it, saying Aarin would be able to invest at least $200,000 (Rs 1.2 crore) and that we should target about $600,000 (Rs 3.6 crore) total for the bridge round. Just now, Usha had basically committed Rs 1.2 crore from Saha fund to match Aarin's Rs 1.2 crore. I would be happy closing the round with even $400,000 (Rs 2.4 crore); it would buy us at least another twelve months at our current burn rate.

I thanked everyone, closed the meeting, and walked out of the boardroom with my head held high. Things were looking up.

Two weeks later, everything changed.

Chapter Eight

'Investors are pinched by two kinds of fear: fear of investing in startups that fizzle and fear of missing out on startups that take off.'

– Paul Graham

By the middle of October, Deepak told me he had reviewed his commitment and concluded that Aarin could put in $50,000 (Rs 30 lakhs) and Saha would maintain their commitment to match them, meaning another $50,000. Further, they would only make this investment if other investors also ponied up more cash.

In hindsight, it would be a lie to say that I can't see where they were coming from. They had invested a large amount of money, between the main fund, Aarin,

Mohandas's two sons, Pranav and Siddharth, one of Mohandas's friends, Sunil, and now, the female founder fund they were an LP in, Saha fund, would also get involved. All in all, Mohandas Pai's money was heavily invested in my business, and twelve months after meeting me for the first time, my business was not showing great or rapid returns whatsoever.

Investors have reasons for changing their strategy, just like entrepreneurs have reasons for pivoting. Often, when entrepreneurs pivot our product – when we change the main product offering – we leave many users abandoned by our pivot with no notice whatsoever. Users purchase a product or service assuming it will not disappear nor will the customer service line be shut off indefinitely. The reality of starting up a business is that you must sell a vision to everyone – investors, users, teammates – knowing that vision may not come to fruition or may change drastically without any clear reason.

My failure was in believing I was the only 'entrepreneur' in this whole ordeal. I was not. Mohan was also starting up, just like me. He was figuring out his strategy, and I was one of his first shots at early stage investment success. I could blame him and Deepak and Pranav for selling me a lie, but then I'd be leaving out the lies I sold them about the quality of my business.

At the time, I was 100 per cent confident my business would find a way to make money, but I honestly had no idea what that way would be. I thought it could be growing to Bengaluru, it could be hiring more people, it could be taking cash payments, it could be building a merchant dashboard, it could be making the homepage easier to search. I had no idea which combination of ideas would result in the kind of 'hockey-stick' revenue growth I was hoping I would see in our numbers one day. I felt sure I'd figure it out, though.

◈

Over the next three months, things followed a sine wave path. Even though our interns had come and left by July, our core team had grown rapidly since then, and by November, KleverKid's first birthday, we were a team of eighteen.

PK and I had never managed a team this large before though, and we were starting to see cracks in the foundation form. Saif, whom we viewed as the heart of our business, was struggling to grow at the same pace that the company needed him to grow. No matter what new role or project we tried to give him, we weren't seeing him step up to the plate like he once did. PK and I knew we had to make a tough decision about him, and that it could impact the whole company's morale.

Saif was everyone's best friend. He was the first person to show a new hire around Shahpur Jat, introduce them to the chai wallah and tell them the secret locations of the cheapest, yummiest meals in the area. Saif was the guy you pulled aside to ask for advice about your girl troubles, and the guy you whispered your frustration to about how PK and Shab were being unreasonable. Saif was the guy who explained how stressful things could get around here, but that we were a good group and we were all lucky to be here together.

Saif was not the guy you wanted to fire. But we knew we had to, and we knew it would be one of the toughest things we ever did.

Bengaluru was looking like a bust, too. PK and I could tell that Karthik needed more support, but we were barely making things work in Delhi. The Bengaluru 'office' rarely got any of our attention, and no matter how hard he was trying to make it work, Karthik was having the same problems in Bengaluru that we were having in Delhi. It wasn't his fault, but we needed him back in Delhi.

By 31 December, PK reported our CAC, customer acquisition cost, to be $261. Our average transaction size was $8. This meant we were losing $253 on every customer we acquired.

When I read that number, that stark, clear number that showed we were throwing money away by the minute, I cried. For the first time since the day I started this business over one year ago, I had serious doubts about our future. Our success no longer felt inevitable. My success no longer felt inevitable.

◈

By 1 February, Saif was no longer at KleverKid, Karthik was asked to shutdown Bengaluru and move back to Delhi, but declined and unceremoniously quit instead, and the mood at the office was becoming eerily cold and unhappy. People were now leaving at 6 p.m. instead of 10 p.m.

I thought back to the first startup I built in India in 2009, MILLEE, with the professor from Carnegie Mellon University. I was based in Hyderabad while the professor was based in Pittsburgh. We hired students from various colleges to intern with us and help us build educational games that could teach English to fifth graders in rural India.

In 2010, I applied to a fellowship program called The Unreasonable Institute. The program said it was intending to give social entrepreneurs a summer-long mini-MBA crash course on building and sustaining social enterprises. It was based in Boulder, Colorado. Potential fellows would crowd fund their fellowship fees of $6,500, and the first twenty-five fellows to succeed raising the full amount would spend the summer in a fraternity house in Boulder together, meeting mentors, investors and advisors that would ultimately shape our business and 'give it wings'.

I solicited money from everyone I knew, got accepted into the program, and by May 2010, was in Boulder gearing up for the summer of a lifetime. Entrepreneurs from all over the world flew in on day one. We each pitched our businesses in front of a large audience, and secretly compared ourselves against each other. Who had the best idea? Who was going to save the most people? Who was the most confident on stage? Who told the story that made the most people cry?

Then, on 18 June 2010, while I was out partying with my new social entrepreneur friends late into the night in Boulder, I got a call. One of the interns at MILLEE had died.

His name was Manish. He was only twenty-two years old. He was a student at a university in Gujarat at the time but since he had been accepted to a Carnegie Mellon University summer program, he was spending the summer in Pittsburgh while I was in Boulder. Unbeknownst to me, Manish had severe epilepsy. It turned out, Manish was quite regular about taking his medication and managing his seizures, but one night he was working late to get a MILLEE game developed on time, and he hadn't slept properly. Seizures can be very sensitive to sleep patterns.

When Manish got home to his dorm room late into the night, he went to the bathroom, and he had a seizure. He hit his head during the seizure, and never recovered. My body went ice cold when I heard the news.

In hindsight, I can convince myself this was not directly my fault, but at the time, I was sure I had a hand in Manish's death. I was hard on my team and strict with them about meeting deadlines, regardless of whatever else was going on in their lives. I can tell myself that, had I known, I would have been more careful with Manish and his health, but the truth is that everyone has a life outside of work that can be overwhelming to balance with a demanding workload and a tough CEO.

◈

Maybe it's better that my KleverKid team is leaving earlier these days, I told myself in Delhi in early 2016. *Maybe they're just balancing out their lives, staying healthy, and getting some rest*, I thought.

Aarin, Saha, and one existing angel investor, Rakesh, finally agreed to each invest $75,000 (Rs 45 lakhs) in our bridge round – a round that 'bridges' a company with a bit of extra capital, without conducting the more painful legalities and formalities of pricing the business, from one series letter to the next – buying us another seven to nine months of runway before we had to raise our Series A. There was no way we'd reach profitability by then, so I knew I'd have to start fundraising for our Series A right away to set us up for a couple more years' worth of growth and sustenance.

I wasn't sure if I could do this one more time. It felt like I was constantly in fundraising mode, and my heart, body and mental health were starting to feel the effects. What I told the outside world was that we were succeeding, but inside, I was coming apart at the seams.

Chapter Nine

'There is a huge amount of pressure as a founder to never show weakness and to be the cheerleader in all internal and external situations. The world can be falling down around you – and most of the time when you're running a company, it is – and you have to be the strong, confident, and optimistic (one). Failing is terrifying...'
— Sam Altman

By March 2016, I decided I'd peg our Series A raise at Rs 30 crore; five million dollars. Investors and funds often require a 'minimum ticket size' to consider a business for funding. Five million was a common minimum ticket size at the time in India. I could also finagle the financial model and capitalization table to make the business look like it was worth about five times that much money. That meant that I could offer a 20 per cent stake in my business to a fund investing five million dollars.

This, I knew even then, would be a very aggressive pitch. It meant that I believed our business valuation had grown from $1 million to $25 million – in under two years. We still didn't have sustainable revenue figured out, but I told myself that this is what all founders had to do to survive. Bite your tongue, pinch your nose and jump back in, I told myself. It will all work out.

I spent the month of March trying to patch up the culture problems inside our company by spending more time at the office, working with the team and boosting morale. That meant more social events with Kingfisher beer, more lavish birthday cakes, and more rah-rah-ing everyone's small wins. Less bemoaning of people's failures.

Often when other people failed, I would publicize it, but when I failed, I would hide it. Like when the Uber partnership failed. It popped and then fizzled out, like most partnerships did. I was starting to notice that 'partnership' was just a fancy term people used for accessing another company's users. No partnership came without its fair share of an eye for an eye trading of user data. Few of us blatantly sold user information, but at the end of the day, that's what it was.

In April, I started fundraising one more time. This time, I reached out to my existing investors and asked them for introductions. We'd be raising a larger round this time, so we had to approach institutionalized investors, not the angel and seed investors we had already approached in past rounds. Often small fish knew big fish in the same pond.

Of course, there were still many open questions inside the business. Our CAC, cost to acquire a customer, was finally below $50 per customer, and our LTV, lifetime value, was slightly above $50 per customer. However, LTV is just a magical number you hope to be true in the early days until you can prove it. We were still feeling around in the dark with our LTV, and I had no idea if one-time-customers would eventually become lifetime customers that continued to book classes through us. If the Uber exec was right, it could take a full year between the first and second class booked by one customer before we would know if we had acquired a 'lifetime' customer.

We had pulled back all our resources and investments outside of Delhi though, and we were entirely focused on solving the unit economics equation in Delhi before we tried growing to a new city again.

Delhi was starting to look better by April. For the entire history of the business, I had declined requests from advertisers to display their ads to our users. We had various companies reach out to us – we had a strong user base of parents and many product companies targeted parents as their primary buyer. Companies selling toys, games, baby food, kid's clothing, etc., would all pay a hefty fee just to display their ads on our website. I was vehement about the sanctity of our product, and until April, I refused to let these types of ads creep onto our site and ruin the user experience. This is an educational website, I would tell my team. Ads would commercialize it, and parents would never come back.

Then, in April, just as I started fundraising again, we became desperate. We needed to show some kind of revenue that was sizeable and scalable, so I told PK to open up ad revenue to prospective clients just to see what the response was like. PK put Shivani and her team on the project, and the minute they made a few calls, they had offers in the door. Companies were willing to pay thousands of dollars to advertise on our website and apps. People wanted to generate leads for their products through our website. Overnight, we became a tiny version of the Parent's Facebook, and it was all delayed due to my own foolish stubbornness.

When I think about the year and a half that passed before I opened the door to ad revenue, I feel a deep sense of regret. We had a huge opportunity to provide a marketplace service that was free to both merchants and users, while charging advertisers to promote their products through us. But I waited too long, and I acted too righteous about an assumption that turned out not to be true.

Parents actually enjoyed seeing relevant ads. When they clicked on a cricket class, we displayed cricket clothing. When they clicked on a music class, we displayed instruments. When they clicked on a summer camp, we displayed summer clothes and games. We could even display vacation packages that were specifically catered to families. The ads didn't bother them at all.

As June came around the corner, our revenue was finally hitting its stride. We had closed $5,000 (Rs 3 lakh) in ad revenue in May alone. Although we were still burning nearly $25,000 (Rs 15 lakh) every month, this was an incredible feat for our team. We finally had a good reason to celebrate.

I gathered the team and gave a long speech. I knew they had been working hard to get to this point, but they were feeling exhausted and let down by me. Although our revenue was finally looking up, I was worried I was starting to lose their faith in my leadership and vision. I imagined we might have a difficult road ahead of us still – our revenue was growing but it would not be enough to delay fundraising our Series A, which meant I would be away from the office for long periods again in the upcoming months.

'Dear Superheroes,' I said.

'I come to you with my head in my hands and my heart feeling like a shattered glass vase on the floor. I have failed you guys miserably recently. In the last three months, I have made numerous mistakes that I am so, so, sorry for.

'Many of you joined this "family" for one reason: you cared about making a difference in the world. That's also why I started this company. I started with a vision of giving kids the best teachers that exist. I started with the hope that we, a small group of believers, could affect the education system for kids just like us.

'In a time when our business was just a baby learning to speak and crawl, I demanded that she run and jump. In a time when we faced extreme outside pressure from investor demands, I crumbled and passed that pressure and stress down to each of you. In a time when you needed a leader, I became a follower.

'I have struggled in the past three months to stare adversity in the face and overcome it with my gumption and passion. I know, and I can feel, that many of you have faced similar struggles. You have worked hard to keep those beautiful smiles on your faces even when your hard work went unnoticed. You have maintained a strong connection to your teammates even when your managers have changed the plan for you, day on day, week on week. You have managed to try and hit your targets every month without taking breaks, without taking time off with your families and friends, because you still believe in what we're doing, even though it's really hard and things seem bleak and scary at times. You have been brave through a rough time when I have made you fear for your jobs and our future together. I am so proud of each of you for sticking it out this far and for believing in the power of what we are building.

'When I lived in Cambodia I met a young woman on the street outside my apartment. Her name was Keda. One day, she told me that she grew up in a village outside of Phnom Penh. Her mom struggled to make ends meet for the family, and her dad had left them years back. One day when a man visited her home and spoke with her mom for a while, everything changed for Keda. The next thing she knew, Keda was in the back of this man's truck leaving her village and headed to Phnom Penh. Keda spent the next three years locked in a room, forced to have sex with random men. At times, someone would come into her cell and inject her with drugs so that she would stop fighting off the men and succumb to their will. Then, one day, she found the door to her cell was unlocked. She ran and ran. She lived on the street and begged for food. She hid at the back of a bookstore one day, pretending to read for hours until the owner told her she either needed to get lost or help him sell books. She told him she could not read but she would be willing to do any respectable work he asked of her. The man gave her a cart and a few books and told her to go to the street and try and sell them. At the end of every day he would teach her to read as repayment. She slowly learnt English that way, and by the time I met her, she was not only selling me a new book every day, but she was speaking fluent English as well. Now she's married, she lives in the UK with a man she loves, she has a great job, and she pings me on Facebook every so often to tell me about how her life has changed all because of one incredible person who was her teacher and mentor.

'I'm telling you this story for two reasons.

'One, no matter how difficult things are getting for us personally and as a team, it's important for us to remember the kids out there whose lives could be completely changed because of one amazing teacher.

'Two, because kids like Keda are the real reason we exist: we're not here to make billions of dollars and we're not here to help crazy wealthy tiger moms put their kids into a hundred classes just to occupy their kids away from the home. We're here to make a difference that could change people's lives and our country as a whole.

'I believe we have the ability to help more kids like Keda, and I'm sorry I've led each of you to a path that forgot about the real reason we're here. I let myself get carried away by what was expected of us, rather than follow the light of what we expect of ourselves.

'I promise I will make a LOT more mistakes in the coming weeks, months and years as we continue to grow and morph. We each know that in an effort to change the world we have to fix some of our broken links and clean up the potholes in our own neighbourhood first. What I am committing to you right now is to bring it back to the original vision and mission. If you catch me being an asshole, bringing everyone down or not following the ethos we've set for ourselves, please just come and tap me on the shoulder and tell me what you think.

'I love you guys a lot and I believe in you tremendously. I'm sorry and I hope you'll forgive me for my missteps. I also hope you still believe in what we're doing enough to stick it out through these rough waters and come out the other side triumphant.'

◈

The entire team was silent after I finished my speech, like the eerie calm before the yearly monsoons hit. It seemed like they were scared and frustrated and needed to see it to believe it. They had given up a lot to be there, and they were tired of my soliloquies.

I truly believed we would come out the other side successful. I could see it no other way. As an entrepreneur, you have no choice but to, somewhat naively at times, believe you have the ability to overcome all the obstacles that fall in your way. That's why you chose to build a company in the first place. You started with the intention to create something and succeed, and since you have always completed everything you started, you can see no end other than success.

At this specific moment in the history of our company, we were doing fairly well, much better than we had ever done in the past. We had a revenue model that finally worked, and we had a plan to grow such that we could become self-sustainable within two years; no small feat for an early stage marketplace startup.

My life was a bit of a wreck, though. I had this deep tension inside of me that I couldn't clearly elucidate at the time, but that started to eat away at me like a cancer to my heart.

◈

An hour later I stooped down to lift a twenty-litre bottle of water to place on top of an old rickety wooden stool. We used the stool as a makeshift shelf for dispensing filtered drinking water in our office.

It happened in slow motion. I bent over, putting my weight in my toes. I grabbed the neck of the jug with my right hand, tilted it over slightly and slid my left hand under the heavy belly. The water sloshed inside the jug, shifting the weight from side to side. As I started to lift, my hips fell a few inches, my knees bent under the weight and my back rounded. I lifted a little more, sitting into an awkward half-squat like a foreigner trying to use a toilet in the developing world for the first time. Suddenly, my body jerked up in reflex, straightening my back, overcompensating. I heard a sharp sound, like a tree snapping in the wind.

Like a fragile, ailing old grandmother ready to be sent to the nursing home and never visited again, I threw my back out in front of my entire team.

First, my vision went blurry, then completely dark. I dropped the jug on its side, lukewarm water pooled around my feet, wetting my canvas flats. My left hand searched for something to steady myself; a wall, a shelf, a table, a chair. My right hand fumbled at my spine where it met my hips. My knees buckled under me. The pain was excruciating, sending waves of lava through my veins and melting my muscles. Someone's voice echoed in my ear, but nothing made sense. My mouth tasted like old copper pennies.

What seemed like hours later, my vision started to clear. Ten sets of eyes peered down at me, searching for signs of life.

'I'm OK. Don't worry.' I whispered.

'What happened?'

'My back. Not sure. Get ice.'

'Can you move?'

'I don't know. I don't think so.'

'Want a doctor? Meds? WebMD?'

'No, no, no. Just ice.'

I laid flat on my back on the wet floor in the middle of my office. I stared up at a disgusting ceiling fan that hadn't been cleaned in over a year, watching a large clump of dust and dead hair spin around and around, gather momentum, and teeter further towards the edge by the second. I knew that when it fell from that fan to my face, I wouldn't be able to do a thing about it: I could not move.

While my brain was gearing up to raise millions of dollars to keep my business alive, my body was telling me I had to stop. I needed a break.

Chapter 10

'You have to give to receive. You have to surrender to something outside yourself to gain strength within yourself. You have to conquer your desire to get what you crave. Success leads to the greatest failure, which is pride. Failure leads to the greatest success, which is humility and learning. In order to fulfil yourself, you have to forget yourself. In order to find yourself, you have to lose yourself.'

– David Brooks, *The Road to Character*

I felt like a fearful child who was playing hide-and-seek with her alter ego for years. Sometimes I was winning; she was It. I ran and ducked and hid and waited to see if she'd find me while I bit down on my fingernails and scanned left and right for signs of her. When I found a great hiding spot, I'd chuckle to myself as I watched her skip past me, convinced I'd duped her once again. Most of the time, though, she was winning; I was It. I'd run after her, but she was faster than me, cleverer than me. It took everything I had inside of me to find her. It happened rarely. Only this time, I had accidentally bumped into her as I stumbled backwards from the harsh blow of falling. In my mind, as I lay on the ground of my office staring at the ceiling fan, I could see my alter ego peering over at me, looking me straight in the eyes. This time, she wasn't running away, and neither could I. The games between us were over. It was time to have an honest conversation.

The games between my alter ego and I began nine years prior. It was the fall of 2008. I was twenty-three years old. I sat in my cushioned swivel chair on the thirty-second floor of a drab grey building on Wall Street, staring at a blank Excel spreadsheet. An email notification appeared at the bottom right corner of my screen every five minutes reading, 'Send the project timeline ASAP!' Each time, I watched it fade away as if it were giving up.

I wondered how long it would take to stand up from my desk, walk to the stairwell, walk down thirty-two flights of stairs, exit the building, buy a small cup of coffee, drink the small cup of coffee, walk back to my building, walk back up thirty-two flights of stairs and sit back down at my desk. If I could stretch it to exactly forty-three minutes, I could leave for the day without responding to the email.

It seemed impossible to get fired from your job on Wall Street in those days. I was hired out of college from Carnegie Mellon University in May of 2007, just before the subprime mortgage crisis began in December the same year. Luckily, I was not hired to work on collateralized debt obligations (CDOs). As it turned out, CDOs were being created, inflated and traded by bankers at many wall street firms including my employer, Merrill Lynch. These shady CDOs eventually led to the demise and ultimate shut down of a handful of companies, as well as the recession and painful loss of nine million people's jobs and seven million people's homes.

When I saw the damage being done over a year into the job, I knew I was not directly responsible, but I knew I was not innocent either. I felt like I was sitting in the back seat of a demolition truck, quietly observing and nodding along with my hands folded in my lap as the driver bulldozed over millions of people's homes and lives.

I didn't know how to stop it; I was one of 60,000 bystanders, all employees of the large and established financial institution, Merrill Lynch. But I knew I had to get out of the back seat. I couldn't imagine looking back on my life in fifty years and feeling proud of myself for sticking around just because the job title looked good and it paid well.

I wasn't raised to just quit my job without a backup plan though. I was raised to play it safe, to plan for the future and to always have at least three months' rent ready for an emergency. In fact, the only reason I was in this job on Wall Street rather than working in a village in Kenya with the Peace Corps was because I was raised to, and expected to, play it safe.

'You can go save the world after you spend some time in a real job learning some real skills in the real world,' Dad said. 'You wouldn't survive in a village, anyways. You're too spoiled.' After working in the 'real world' for one year, with a lifetime of college debt still to pay off, it felt like my options were limited. I couldn't just find a new job out of thin air. I would have to stay, for now, I decided.

A small voice grew like a tumour inside me, harmless at first. It was my alter ego. She asked if I was happy. She asked if I was having fun. I answered I was having fun but I wasn't sure if I was happy. Honestly, I didn't know what 'happiness' meant. Dad would say, 'Happiness is for the hippies.'

The voice grew louder day-by-day. She became unrelenting. No matter what I did to shut her up, she grew louder, stronger, deeper. She latched onto my bones. She took on a life of her own. As the weeks and months went by, it became impossible to ignore her.

'Do you even care what you do with your life? Do you want to make a difference? Can't you tell you are resting on your laurels, wasting time? Are you waiting for someone to give you permission?' she asked.

'Yes,' I said. 'Yes.'

'You don't need permission from anybody,' she said.

'What will I do?'

'Something that matters.'

'What if I fail?'

'Then you fail,' she said, 'You aren't going to blame that on anyone else. Permission or not.'

'What if it hurts?'

'It will hurt, no doubt about it. Then you'll mend. You'll get back up. Dust off. Try again.'

'What if people judge me?'

'Fuck 'em.'

I quit my job and left America for Cambodia the next month.

I thought back to that first conversation with my alter ego like the first time I saw the ocean. I walked down towards the shimmering blue and along the way I removed my shoes to let my toes melt into the hot sand. I approached the edge of the water, stopped and just stared. It was immense, enticing and it made me so nervous, I cried. I wanted to jump in, but what if I drowned?

◈

Someone from my team called Jonathan to peel me off the office floor and carry me home to our apartment in Safdarjung Enclave a few hours later, when it looked like things weren't getting any better.

Jonathan came to get me from my office, took me home, and laid me out on the floor of our apartment next to my phone and laptop.

'Why don't you try to get some rest instead of working for a little bit?' he said.

'Can you grab me the ibuprofen?'

'I can call Dr Nair, maybe he can diagnose you over the phone. What even happened?'

'I don't know. Whatever, just get me the ibuprofen and my laptop charger, please.'

'You're so stubborn,' he said, and walked off.

◈

After a few hours of lying on the stone floor of our apartment, unable to turn to read or use my laptop for more than a minute or two, I gave up. My phone had finally died and the charger was too far for me to get to. It was the longest I had gone without answering my email in almost two years.

With nothing to do, I laid back and let my alter ego take over.

She kept replaying the scene over and over in my head, asking me what led to it, and what could have gone so wrong that I didn't even realize I was this frail and broken that, like a matchstick after the fire goes out, I just disintegrated into ashes with the lightest touch.

I puzzled over all the CrossFit and running I had been doing at 6 a.m. with Dhruv, my closest friend in Delhi and one of the only other startup founders I knew who actually got me. He got why I did this. He got why I couldn't possibly do anything else. He got why I couldn't give up, regardless of how hard and bleak things may have looked. He also got why CrossFit felt so good, so necessary for people like us.

It wasn't about the workout for us so much as it was about that small slice of the day when, finally, someone other than us, oversaw everything, and there was no need to push back on them or fight them. They did know best, and we felt good letting them take the reins. Someone else called the shots, someone else ordered us around, and someone else was responsible for our health, success and happiness. It felt like coming up for a breath of air before going underwater again for the rest of the day.

While I laid there, I thought about how peculiar it was that the daily transfer from mental and emotional pain to an hour of physical pain helped us cope with it all. It helped us survive. Until it could no longer handle every single thing we threw at it.

My journal sat on the bottom rung of the coffee table next to me. I grabbed it and flipped it open to a recent page. I read the piece out loud as if my alter ego was sitting next to me, waiting patiently with her arms crossed in front of her chest.

'I'm in an airplane right now,' I read. 'The world never stops when I disconnect, as I always believe it should. I am so tightly wound up with everything that is happening around me and everyone who needs me at any given time. Every little notification and alert calls me to change course, to react in some way. With every buzz of the phone, with every sound that screams out loud for attention, I am pulled from one side of my brain to the other. It feels like a tug of war, only there are 10,000 different ropes and everyone is pulling at different moments in different directions, begging me to focus and listen to their specific request.

'But my ears are plugged. They whir with a constant high-pitched tone, like the noise of the air conditioner in the window, drowning every outside sound out.

'I haven't slept properly in days. I wake up at 1 a.m., I lie in bed with constant questions: Is this investor going to write back to me? Will they send me favourable terms? Am I the right person to run and grow this company? Should I call it quits now? When will I stop feeling like a failure?

'I turn the TV on every night because I can't handle the answers that sit right behind that constant whir. I can hear her trying to yell above it all. I can't let the whirring stop.

'But I can't avoid the feeling that it's all been for nothing. That I'm going to have left the children and India with nothing. It drives me crazy – the idea that I've spent so long on a problem and gotten almost nowhere. It's been almost nine years since I moved to India to fix education for kids. What a waste.

'I guess I'll have to choose to forgive myself someday – to recognize that the journey was valuable and the progress, in the end, was not only about the kids. It was about the team. It was about the ideas. It was about the progress of India herself. It was about the innovation. It was about my own education. About understanding the world and business in a completely different light. It was about getting a bunch of people together to tackle a problem in a new and different way. I'll have to accept that we succeeded at some things and we failed at others, but all in all we left a net positive impact on the world, and that is not so bad.

'Is it really over already though? Am I giving up? This can't be the end. I have to give it one last shot. I have to give it everything I've got until there's nothing left.'

I laid the journal down on the floor next to me and closed my eyes. Perhaps it was the medication, the pain, or just the exhaustion, but I lapsed into a deep and dark sleep that held me tight inside its abyss through the next day.

◈

When I woke up, I rolled over and inched like a centipede over to my laptop. I had to write to a few more investors. I had to give this one last shot. My team deserved at least that much from me, after everything they had sacrificed for me.

I wrote up an audacious email to a friend in Silicon Valley whose fund, Learn Capital, made investments in education companies focused on the US market. Were they looking at India yet? If not, it's time they start. We're ripe for the picking, I said. The time is now. And my company should be your first investment here. We're raising $1.5-2 million and need to close in the next three months. Do you want in?

I couldn't ask for $5 million with this guy. He knew my company too well, and besides, his firm didn't have a minimum requirement, so there was no need to high ball him.

I read the email over and over and thought about how absurd this would still sound to my friend, Michael. I was some distant acquaintance, in a barely developed city half-way around the world, asking him to invest millions of dollars into her barely proven business. But, as Dad would say, I was up shit creek without a paddle, and this was my cocky cry for help. I justified to myself that Michael was not an old Indian male investor, so he would be more upfront with me, he would give it to me straight, and he would not treat me like some inferior species that had landed on his planet asking for alms to take back to the mothership.

Michael wrote back immediately. Let's chat, he said. I'll include another partner, Luis, and our managing partner on the call. We are interested.

I asked him when. One week passed. Then two. I emailed him again. Let's talk in two weeks, Michael said. It's been busy around here, our managing partner has been hard to nail down.

Of course, Michael was not the only investor I was talking to at this point in June 2016, but he was the furthest along in my pipeline, and I trusted him the most. Although that's not saying much. By this point, in the midst of my third fundraising round, having talked to over 100 different investors and funds, having worked with ten of them closely as investors in my company, and having the insider knowledge of Jonathan's time as an investor, one who worked with plenty of other investors to finalize terms and close deals, I vehemently distrusted anything investors said to me about investing in my business until they gave me something signed on a physical piece of shiny, white paper.

Until now, I had also been approaching investors with relative ease. Usually my tactic, in my opinion, was calm, patient and gracious. Give them everything they want, have as many conversations as they need, and eventually they will invest, I said to myself. But that didn't turn out well for me in the past. Investors would take my deck, my financial model, my growth plan, ask me hundreds of questions and then turn around and invest their capital in my biggest competitors, using my data against me. Investors would invite me to meet five or six of their associates, one by one, who were about twenty-one or twenty-two years old, fresh out of IIT, who would practice their interview method on me, and then disappear without ever telling me why. They would just stop responding to my emails. It turned out, investors ghosted entrepreneurs *all the time*.

This time I was not going down without a fight. I thought about the time, when I was living in New York City in 2008, I stumbled upon a grungy old boxing gym near my office called Trinity Boxing Club one day. I stalked around the gym for a while, peeking into the windows and pretending to look for some other place before meekly entering the front door. A weathered, dreary eyed, massive white man stood behind the counter, watching me, waiting.

'Can I help you?' he demanded with a strong New Jersey lilt.

'Um, yea, what is this place?'

'A gym.'

'Do you take anyone? Or only professionals?'

'Anyone who wants to fight.'

'So, even someone...like...me?'

'Yea, even someone like you. You want to fight?'

'Yea. I do.'

'It takes commitment, you know. You gotta work hard, ain't no giving up in the middle of a fight. Aright?'

I nodded.

'Aright, go get changed and meet me back here in five. I'll wrap your hands so they don't bleed.'

I ran down to change. From that day forward for the next six months, I spent 6–10 hours every week practising jump rope, building my strength and agility on the fast bags, moving my feet, learning to jab, hook, slip and roll, sprinting around the block and fighting in the ring for three-minute intervals with one-minute breaks in between.

Once, at the start of my first real fight in the ring, my coach started yelling at me from ringside. 'Get in there, Shab! You can't dance around her the entire time. You can't avoid her! You have to throw some punches. You gotta fight her. Get AT her!'

I did. She slipped under my right arm and knocked me out with one swift punch to my jaw. I fell to the ground in slow-motion the way you see in Bugs Bunny cartoons as a kid. I held back tears. When I got up again, people had gathered around the ring, and they were cheering for me. I threw another punch at my opponent. She ducked and hit me with a hook to my side. I crumbled. When were these three fucking minutes going to be over? I got back up in her face and started to dance around, waiting for her to throw a punch that I could block or slip and hit back on. She threw, I rolled and I hit her squarely under her left jaw with my uppercut punch. She stumbled back. That time, too, I felt a wave of hot lava course through my veins, but that time it lit me up. Then the bell rang. Three minutes were up.

◈

By this point, my back had recovered from the fall in the office and I was feeling strong again. I sent Michael my uppercut.

Are you serious about investing in India? I said. If so, I need to know now. I can't wait around forever, I told him. We don't have an infinite amount of runway, and this ship is sailing with or without you.

We're interested, he said. We're not 100 per cent sure about investing in India but we are keen to invest in KleverKid, so there's some convincing that needs to happen with various investment committee members. Hopefully we'll have a decision soon, he said.

To me, this was both encouraging and deflating. What did this even mean?

By the time Michael and I had gone back and forth over email, Skype calls, and WhatsApp texts discussing financial models, capitalization tables, detailed growth plans, and other investors who could participate in the round, we were in the middle of July. I had less than two months' worth of runway left in the bank.

Then, Michael said he was still interested, but they couldn't lead. They needed an Indian investor to lead. Did I have anyone that could lead?

The only investor I knew that could potentially lead at short notice, as long as a marquee investor like Learn Capital would join, was Aarin Capital. I really did not want to go to them again, but I had no options left. I introduced the two funds and held my breath for the outcome.

In the meantime, PK and I had another team crisis on our hands inside the business. We were finally making solid revenue every week, but we needed to let go of our head of merchant sales, Umesh.

Almost no revenue was coming in from our sales to merchants. In our business, the 'merchants' were the kid-focused educational businesses that were listed on our marketplace platform. When we listed a merchant on our platform, it was free, but we also tried to upsell them on purchasing value-added-services from us at the same time. This was supposed to be the scalable side of our revenue model. We had over 10,000 merchants already listed on our platform by this point. If each of them paid us even $2 per month for value added services, we could be covering our entire team's salaries with that income.

The problem was that a majority of these merchants were operating on extremely thin, if any at all, margins. They often started the merchant programmes out of a deep passion for their talent, and a desire to share their passion and talent with children. They were extremely savvy educational micro-entrepreneurs who had opened one or two classrooms over the course of five to ten years, on average. Usually, almost 100 per cent of our merchants' clients heard about their programme through word of mouth from other parents. Any online ads, radio ads, or flyer marketing they had tried in the past had reduced their margins even more, and ultimately failed to return on their investment. This made our merchants extremely difficult, if not impossible, to sell to. They loved being listed on our platform, but they just couldn't pay for it.

All our revenue by this point was coming from the marketing team's advertising sales. Our platform was actually perfect for advertisers like Johnson & Johnson and Burger King, who were growing in India and wanted to reach a wider audience of young, professional, busy parents with lots of places to go and things to do. Young parents with crazy schedules were a highly valuable target audience that many advertisers wanted access to.

That's why my marketing team had been so successful at selling advertising campaigns, while my sales team hadn't been able to sell much at all to small merchants with slim margins. It wasn't Umesh's fault; I misread the merchant market's willingness to pay, and I hired him for a role that I could no longer justify.

There was one big challenge in firing Umesh. His best friend from college, Shivani, was now our head of marketing. PK and I hired both of them on the same day, gave them identical packages and promoted them at the same time. They had been on similar trajectories until this point, and they were both incredible people that the whole team, including PK and I, had become close with.

PK and I had a feeling that if we let go of Umesh, Shivani might become demotivated and despondent, as the two of them had become incredibly close.

'She might even quit,' PK said.

'I don't think she would quit. She's doing so well on ad sales, managing her team, and learning new things every day,' I said.

'I'm not sure; she's very loyal to KleverKid, but who will ultimately win her loyalty? Umesh or us? What will we do if she quits?'

'I don't know. We'd be screwed. We need her. She's bringing in a majority of our ad sales.'

'Then maybe we shouldn't let go of Umesh,' PK said.

'We can't afford him anymore. There's no way to justify his role. Our merchants aren't changing their behaviour any time soon,' I said.

'He will still take it personally, and so will she.'

'I guess we'll just have to wait and see,' I said.

PK and I told Umesh he was being let go the next day, and two hours later, Shivani resigned, too. Within a span of two hours, we lost two of the most experienced, loved and respected managers in the company. And now we'd have to explain it to the rest of the team.

To make things even worse, until this point I had consistently been feeding PK and the entire team the lie that things were looking great for our Series A investment round. We had less than two months of runway in the bank with barely one prospect for an investor in the pipeline.

Things were not looking great at all.

In hindsight, I still believe this is what my team needed to hear to power forward and stay focused. Startups are tough, scary, and filled with unknowns. It's an unnecessary burden to be told by your CEO that she is not sure where your salary is going to come from in two months, but that you should still stay focused on your task at hand and work until the wee hours of the morning.

I imagine most CEOs deal with this problem in their own unique ways, but if I had to do it all over again, I would still tell my team that their jobs were safe until I was confident they were not anymore. My job as CEO was to rally, to inspire and to lead.

◈

Towards the end of July, the Learn Capital folks had been in touch with the Aarin folks. The goal was to try and convince all the parties to agree to terms on the Series A round, encourage Aarin to 'lead' from India, and finally give me something in writing that I could rely on. Something I could hang my hat on and go back to my team with, with my head held high holding Kingfisher beer in celebration.

◈

On 29 July, I held an emergency board meeting to discuss our situation. Revenues were up. Burn rate was down. Expensive people had been let go. EBITDA was on plan. The class discovery tool on our product had been optimized and automated. Our NPS (net promoter score) was high. But, our runway was too short to take long-term bets. We couldn't invest in marketing tests, we couldn't hire smart and experienced people, we couldn't take risks. Our revenue wasn't coming from where we thought it would come from.

We hadn't locked down an A round investor yet, and our pipeline had dried up. We had under two months of runway left. What do you think we should do? I asked.

I opened the table up to the board members.

Deepak asked about the future of the business, 'In the off chance that you did raise your A round, how would you grow?'

'Online, on-demand classes, advertising revenue and integrating products into our services marketplace,' I said.

'What are your daily active users (DAU) at now?' Deepak asked.

'3K DAU,' I said.

'What's your pitch to advertisers?'

'The CAC with us will be higher than FB and Google, but the quality of our leads are much better than theirs. More targeted, more focused, higher likelihood to convert.'

'How much do you charge per lead?'

'200-300 INR/lead,' I said. 'I'm happy to discuss these details more, but I think we should discuss our funding situation first,' I said. 'Last we spoke, Aarin and Saha said they could commit to $250,000 on top of the $1 million that Learn Capital would put in, and Aarin would lead. Then Aarin and Saha came back with a $100,000 offer. Where do we stand on that agreement now that you've talked to Learn Capital?'

Uma chimed in in support of my plan. 'She needs to grow to more markets, and she needs more money to grow her traffic. We need to help her out with more cash.'

'The reality,' Deepak said to the other board members, 'is that Shabnam only has 1–2 months of money left. If no one can lead Learn Capital's investment from India, we're at the end of the road with this company. But I'm quite sure we'll figure something out for her,' he said. 'I'll get back to you all by Monday on where Aarin and Saha stands.'

By Monday, 1 August, he had gotten back to me. Aarin and Saha wouldn't invest anymore in KleverKid, and thus, Learn Capital wouldn't invest in KleverKid, and thus, we were coming to the end of our road.

◈

Although I had held my breath and crossed my fingers and toes and prayed to anyone who might listen for this money to come through, I felt a surprising sense of relief when I heard this news. This meant the death of my baby; the demise of my sweat and blood, the last chapter of my carefully selected and trained and wonderfully courageous team, and it was the end of our journey, but it also meant I could finally stop holding my breath. I had failed the final, most important test I had ever taken. I was a failure.

◈

I called PK the next day to meet with me outside of the office at a nearby café in Shahpur Jat I used as my go-to spot for alone time and peace and quiet from the office, called Ivy & Bean. It was where I did my best thinking. The waiters all knew me by name and brought me my standard order, a beetroot burger and a strong cappuccino, without even asking.

PK walked in the door and sat down next to me. I hadn't touched my food and the cappuccino had gone cold.

'It's over,' I said.

'What do you mean? What did the board say?' PK asked, indignant.

'They won't put more money in. And Learn Capital won't do it without them. We're out of options.'

'It can't be. There has to be some other way. What about the other investors? Round Glass? Sequoia?'

'Round Glass invested in BabyChakra, our biggest competitor. Sequoia isn't returning my calls. This is it, PK. I'm so sorry. I've totally failed you.'

'Wow. I can't believe it. I had no idea. I thought you were going to tell me that you closed the round.'

'I know. I wished for that, too. Listen, I don't want to drag this out to the last second and leave our team out to dry with no options. We still have a little more than a month of money in the bank. Let's put a plan together, and tell the team sooner than later, that way we can help them find jobs through our network and even give them some severance pay. Maybe we can give them their raises now so that their next jobs match to higher salaries too.'

'Yea, we should do that. They've deserved raises for months now. They've all worked so hard. This is going to be a rough few weeks.'

'I know. I'm really sorry.'

PK and I sat in silence for an hour together. Over the two years we spent working together, we had never spent that much time saying absolutely nothing to one another.

◈

On Thursday, 4 August, I read my speech to the KleverKid team. I sent the same note to all my investors, advisors and supporters. I took one deep, long breath, and then, I cried.

Epilogue

'I couldn't wait for success,
so I went ahead without it.'
– Jonathan Winters

The first thing that happened after I decided to shut down my business, fire my team and label myself a failure, was the onset of extreme and debilitating panic attacks.

Jonathan had moved from India back to the US to attend a master's program in Cambridge and all his stuff was gone from our apartment, so I was alone for the first time in a long time. Many of my friends had left India to pursue other opportunities, so I was by myself with no one to call. At least, no one to call that I actually wanted to talk to, or admit to, what was happening.

I felt like I had come completely undone. Every few minutes it felt like I could not breathe. I would get an ache in my chest and my breathing would shorten. I would try to take small sips of air but my breathing would only get worse and I would get more scared. I tried to stand with my back against a wall or lay down flat on the ground or even scream into a pillow but nothing helped. I tried drinking too much red wine in the middle of the day but I didn't feel that sweet light buzz and my breathing only worsened. I wanted to get rid of this pain in some way, but I couldn't.

Someone recommended meditation, so I downloaded the Headspace app onto my phone. I could focus for a few seconds on the man doing the meditation but then I'd lapse back into anxiety and breathlessness when I thought about how stupid I was and what a waste of time this was and how I lost everyone's money.

What would I do next? Who would hire me? Who would want my spoiled goods of a brain and a career? What did I know? I knew nothing. I had wasted ten years of my career trying to be different. Was I trying to prove something? Well, I sure showed them, didn't I? What will Dad say? What will I tell him?

I hadn't kept in touch with my parents over the final year of running KleverKid. I tried to put placeholder meetings in my calendar to remind me to call them once a week, but I always skipped it and told myself I'd do it the following week, but I never did. Sometimes they'd call, but I'd rarely answer. If I did, I would rush them off the line and tell them I'd call them back later. I was avoiding them.

It wasn't until this moment in August of 2016 that I finally understood why. I was failing, and I was ashamed. I couldn't face them. My success was supposed to be inevitable. But it seemed like failure was all that was truly inevitable in my life.

I flew to LA for my cousin's wedding, and I sat my parents down in the hotel room to tell them what was going on.

'I'm shutting down my business,' I said. 'I failed.'

'That sounds like the right thing to do, Shabnam. You tried your best. I am proud of you,' Dad said.

'Does this mean you're moving back to the US?' Mom asked.

'Maybe, I'm not sure. I haven't decided yet.'

'Well, it's up to you. We're here for you, you know. You worked really hard, but it was time to call it quits. These things happen,' Dad said.

It wasn't what I expected them to say. I expected them to be disappointed, dismayed and distraught. I expected them to be angry. I had squandered their college education investment. I had squandered their KleverKid investment capital too. I had squandered it all.

Instead, they embraced me. The people I was most afraid and ashamed to admit my failure to were the ones who were the least phased by it. Shit happens, they were saying. Gotta move on.

I left LA feeling a little less anxious about my past but a little more uneasy about my future. I hadn't planned for this, and I had no idea what I would do next. Worse, I hadn't saved a penny over the last ten years of starting companies and paying myself next to nothing.

How would I survive?

Then, I got a call from an unknown number. The woman on the line introduced herself as an editor at HarperCollins. She said she had seen my name in the newspaper and watched a talk of mine from a TEDx recording on YouTube. She said she read through my blog pieces and wanted to know if I had ever thought about writing a book about embracing our fear of failure.

I nearly laughed on the line. The news of my business shutting down was not public yet, so I knew that she had no idea about my latest and greatest failure, but I also wondered how I could possibly write a book about embracing my fear of failure when I was amid the biggest failure of my life, and I was far from embracing myself for it.

In fact, I wanted to erase the last two years of my life, hide under the covers until everyone forgot who I was, and then magically emerge like a butterfly from its cocoon once I had become a brilliant and runway success.

That path would look decidedly different from the one of publishing a book about failure.

Then, as always, the doubt came crashing in to greet me. Why does she want me to write a book? Do I deserve this? Am I worthy of a book deal? What have I done that people would want to read about? Am I going to be any good at this? Is anyone going to read this? Can I live up to my own, this editor's, or anyone else's expectations of me? What if I fail?

Then, I asked myself, if I were to commit to this, what would I need to accomplish this? What would success look like? Maybe success wasn't about the money or the fame for me anymore. Maybe it was about something else. Something less tangible. Maybe success was about how closely I was living my values. Maybe success, for me, was actually about the quality of the journey, rather than the final destination.

I thought about the quality of my journey with KleverKid. It had been such an incredible ride. I had never felt so challenged, so alive, nor so inspired as I was at the KleverKid office every single day. I never knew what to expect walking in the door every morning, and I never felt as accomplished as when I locked up the office at night. The journey had been incredible, even though the destination was not what I had envisioned or expected. And working with my young team to teach them how to take risks, embrace failure and redefine success in their own lives was one of the greatest accomplishments in my life.

Maybe I can write this book, I thought to myself. I think I'd need to focus, to feel safe and to feel loved to write a great book. That meant moving back to America to be with Jonathan, living with him in Cambridge and working on recovering from my failure by writing my book.

I spent the next nine months in deep recovery. Sometimes I woke up at 2 a.m. in a cold sweat, sleep talking about CACs and DAUs and LTVs. Sometimes I woke up at noon and stayed in my pyjamas all day, watching *Friends* reruns. Sometimes I got up the courage to shower, go to the library and write a few pages. Sometimes I turned off my phone and my laptop, deactivated Facebook and Instagram and SnapChat, and listened to music on my old iPod all day. Sometimes I called my Dad.

I had studied, researched and interviewed hundreds of people about their experiences and relationship with failure. I knew what the trajectory would look like for me. As much as I wanted to be different from everyone else, I was just the same. Failure might hurt less or more to certain people, but the trajectory is much the same.

First, I would hit a deep slump of depression, blame, and anger. I would lose my energy and my willpower. I would do everything I could to avoid thinking about what happened, which would make me think about it even more and fall deeper into a hole.

Then, over time, I would start to see the light again. I would start to find ideas compelling, but still not get ignited by them. I would listen, but not act.

Then, eventually, much later, I would discover my creative flow. I would get excited about ideas, I would think about ways I could add value and I would get my hands dirty trying to make things work.

It took me a full two years from the day I announced the shutdown of my business to the day I found my creative flow again. I went through bouts of depression, regret, remorse, blame, listlessness, frustration, pessimism and, worst of all, carelessness. I just stopped caring for a while.

What got me through it, what gets everyone through it I think, is love where I least expected it, hugs when I least wanted them, and the blind faith that I would come out the other side of this a bigger, better person someday.

And, so I did. I don't regret one day of this adventure, this failure, because I know I would be worse off today had I never tried in the first place.

It was all worth it, and I would do it all over again if I had the chance.

Acknowledgements

Jonathan Mazumdar, for your heart and your head and your hugs and your tickles. I am so lucky to have found you in at the back of that 'Jazz club' in Mumbai that day. Thank you for your honesty and your critique. You make me strive to be a better person every day.

Madhu Aggarwal, for giving me life, hope and inspiration. For letting me blame everything in the world on you, and still loving me through it all. Avnish Aggarwal, for everything I am today. You are my best friend and my harshest critic, and I love you for both.

Maria Springer, for being my voice when I felt silenced, for being my ear when I felt unheard, for being my rock when things got shaky and for being a boss when the world said you can't. Priyanka Khanna, for letting me pull you onto this rollercoaster with me, and for staying on it with me until the bitter end. And for all the painful calls you took while I was writing this book, for confirming my fears of what went wrong, and for letting me ask you how I failed. Jessie Arora, for cheering me on through the years, giving me confidence when I was unsure, and for redefining what 'mom' should really mean for women.

Naveen Yogi Aggarwal, for rebuilding, breathing, and teaching me to be better. For your silent support. Shella Aggarwal, for being the calm in the Aggarwal family, and for creating and raising such a good little person that is destined for greatness. Mira Nair, for crying through my dreadful first draft, and for being the only one who really understood. Rashi Birla, for reading so many awful first drafts while travelling the world and living your life, how did I find you? Gauri Kirloskar, for being honest and for challenging me to be better, try harder and live larger. Karthik Chandrashekar, for the office space, the financial models and the unwavering support even when I called your VC friends assholes. Amrisha Prashar, gracias por tu amor, tu amistad y them badass beats. Rukun Kaul, for the laughter, the love and the true definition of friendship. Anjali Grover, for the bitter truth, because you know I can be better. Amy Patel, for rooting for me on and off the field. Ajay Kamat, for keeping and sending me those ridiculous letters, and for giving me Mexico City. Carrie O'Laughlin, for making me laugh when I've most wanted to cry this past year. Jonathan Jackson, for giving me the time, space and encouragement to get this over the finish line. Danny Greenberg (Uncle/Coach), for being a voice of reason in a sea of expectation. Pravat Uncle and Mary Anne, for the wine and the belief that I can make it to the top of this mountain too. Priya Gulati, for being my soul sister, my chudbud and my momspiration. Preeta Rajamani, for not reading a single line of my book, but pretending to and for keeping me humble throughout the process. Dorian, for the astute feedback I needed to hear when my sassy alter ego needed to not be Jamaican. Kim Jaso, for being my first real-life writer friend who moved me to tears and gave me writing to aspire to. Uma, for believing in me, supporting me and always having my back.

Debasri Rakshit, for calling me up out of the blue, for being my first Sherpa and for convincing me to write this book. Shreya Punj, for being a patient editor to a first-time author, I applaud your courage and tenacity. Ananth Padmanabhan, for your friendship and your belief in my work. Thank you.

For all the KleverKids. You were, you are and you will always be my dream team of superheroes. Keep risking it, keep killing it and keep failing.